WOULD YOU RATHER...?

by Justin Heimberg & David Gomberg

An Absolutely Absurd
ANTHOLOGY

ver **3,000 Absolutely Absur... ...emmas** to Ponder

Published by Seven Footer Press
247 West 30th Street
Second Floor
New York, NY 10001

First printing August 2011
10 9 8 7 6 5 4 3 2 1

Would You Rather...? Is a registered trademark
used under license from Spin Master Ltd.

Cover Design by Junko Miyakoshi
Design by Thomas Schirtz

ISBN 978-1-934734-47-6

www.sevenfooterpress.com

Mazel Tov, *Would You Rather...?* !

Thirteen years before the time of this writing, the original *Would You Rather...?* was birthed into this world. It was a light and thin little thing, an easy birth, with few labor pains; the product of a casual dalliance (strictly platonic) between school chums David Gomberg and Justin Heimberg (i.e. us.)

Today, 13 years later, that little baby is becoming a man. Consider the publication of this anthology as *Would You Rather...?*s bar mitzvah, complete with all of the associated awkwardness, juvenile humor, and rabbi references.

Bulkier and of debatably deeper voice, the pubescent *Would You Rather...?* is accordingly thicker (for those of you actually reading a paper book), theoretically wiser—but actually not at all—and completely obsessed with bathroom humor (so some things have not changed.)

So celebrate this special occasion for our little bubbeleh with us by gathering a group of friends, grabbing a glass of Manischewitz, and Hora-ing it up. And don't be afraid to let loose tonight.

Shalom,

Justin and David

Table of Contents

1

Slightly Extreme!

Oh yeah! That's right. These questions aren't for the faint of heart. No way, baby! Woohoooooo! Seniors!!!! However, nor do these questions exceed the daily recommended dosage of extremity (not extreme enough to drop the "E" and spell it X-treme, for instance). First things first. Start by challenging your friends with these quandaries ranging from the slightly extreme to the extremely slightly extreme to the slightly extremely slightly extreme!

Would you rather...

have granola boogers

OR

salt-and-pepper dandruff?

Things to consider: getting hungry on the trail, breakfast on the morning commute

Would you rather...

only be able to enter rooms via Kool-Aid man-style wall crashes

OR

only be able to exit rooms by jumping through a window as if fleeing a burning building?

Things to consider: cheery "Oh Yeah!"'s, panic-laden screams

Would you rather...

have orgasms as loud as a howler monkey

OR

orgasms as gushing as a Mentos dropped in Diet Coke?

YOU MUST CHOOSE!

Would you rather...

fall off a ladder and catch your eyelid on a nail

OR

slide down a banister of razor blades?

Would you rather...

have recess at your office

OR

have nap time?

Would you rather...

spend a minute in one of those glass cases of swirling money but have the dollar bills replaced with pieces of used toilet paper

OR

swim a lap in a pool of 65% urine/35% water?

YOU MUST CHOOSE!

Would you rather...

react like a belligerent drunk when you get frustrated and disappointed

OR

react like a petulant 3-year-old when snubbed by a member of the opposite sex?

Would you rather...

have a type of Tourette's Syndrome where you periodically exclaim "Booyah!"

OR

have a facial tick to the rhythm of the opening bars of "Eye of the Tiger"?

Things to consider: corporate presentations, your wedding ceremony

YOU MUST CHOOSE!

Would you rather...

sneeze a blast of shotgun pellets

OR

pee liquid nitrogen?

Things to consider: crime-fighting, potential for self-mutilation

Would you rather...

have sex with Rosie O'Donnell

OR

assume her physique?

Would you rather...

have to work on a computer from 1980

OR

use a cell phone from 1980?

YOU MUST CHOOSE!

Would you rather...

BE COMPELLED TO ENTER EVERY ROOM BY JUMPING INTO THE DOORWAY WITH AN IMAGINARY PISTOL LIKE THE STAR OF A '70S COP SHOW

OR

INVARIABLY MAKE YOUR ORGASM FACE INSTEAD OF SMILING WHEN BEING PHOTOGRAPHED?

Would you rather...

chisel off your nose

OR

your knee caps?

Would you rather...

have the heart rate of John McCain

OR

the blink rate of John McCain?

Would you rather...

have your child's babysitter be Johnny Knoxville

OR

Paula Abdul?

YOU MUST CHOOSE!

Would you rather...

be able to run a five minute mile but have an absurdly effeminate stride

OR

be able to strut a seven minute mile?

Would you rather...

very slowly sandpaper the skin above your lip completely off

OR

take a BB gun, point it at your top right front tooth, and fire away?

Would you rather...

have a phone app where your phone blinks when someone is lying

OR

have an iDefibrillator app?

YOU MUST CHOOSE!

Ageism... to the Extreme!

Would you rather...

dress like an 80 year-old **OR** walk like one?

have the face of an 80 year-old **OR** have the body of an 80 year-old?

have the face of an 80 year-old **OR** the face of a 2 year-old?

live in a world where we're able to iron our skin wrinkles like clothing **OR** where we continue to lose and gain teeth into adulthood?

age gracefully **OR** never age?

be 25 for your whole life **OR** not?

rust **OR** grow mold as you age?

YOU MUST CHOOSE!

Would you rather...

have your social life restricted to comparing the absorbency of paper towels with middle-aged women like in those commercials

OR

have all your conversations have to in some way incorporate Simón Bolívar?

Things to consider: "That's interesting about your kid's soccer team. Perhaps they will play with the intensity of South American freedom fighter Simón Bolívar."

Would you rather...

only be able to drive on the wrong side of the road

OR

only be able to drive in reverse?

YOU MUST CHOOSE!

Would you rather...

BE STUCK ON A STALLED BUS WITH FORLORN ACCOUNTANTS

OR

NOSY PIRATES?

SLIGHTLY EXTREME!

In order to defeat hostile enemies, would you rather MacGyver things into weapons from...

a 99 cent store **OR** a Bath & Body Works?

a farmer's market **OR** a Hallmark shop?

LensCrafters **OR** Burger King?

Things to consider: Explain your technique.

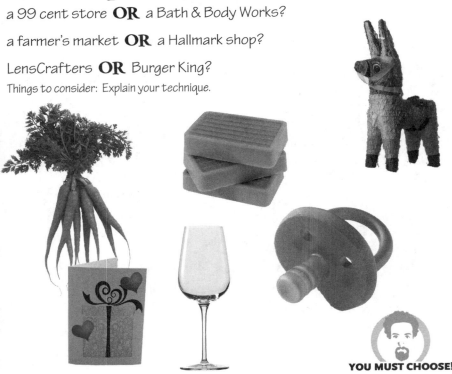

YOU MUST CHOOSE!

Would you rather...

insert a silent "d" in evdery wodrd tdhat dyou tydpe liked tdhis

OR

pronounce a "b" sound before every word you speak, as in "Buh-hi, buh-how, buh-you, buh-doing?"

Would you rather...

have lukewarm vision rays

OR

be able to silence your urinations when going in other people's bathrooms?

Would you rather name your child...

Adolph **OR** Fartsy?

Romulex **OR** Nips?

Destruction Personified **OR** 43?

YOU MUST CHOOSE!

Would you rather...

have poppy-seeded skin

OR

have all of your social interaction carried out at the level of awkwardness and tedium of *Jeopardy* contestant exchanges with Alex Trebek?

Would you rather...

have your feces react to water like Alka-Seltzer

OR

be brown bubbles that float in the air?

YOU MUST CHOOSE!

Would you rather...

have a 48 hour biological clock

OR

a 12 hour biological clock?

Would you rather...

be able to handwrite any font at regular speed

OR

be able to flash a sincere smile on command for photographs?

YOU MUST CHOOSE!

Would you rather...

HAVE MAYONNAISE TEARS

OR

KOOL-AID SWEAT?

Would you rather read...

Pac-Man: The Novel

(Excerpt): Ever-chomping, Pac-Man fled, his mind a blur of dots and darkness. He was operating on instinct now, navigating the labyrinthine hell with a madness to match the situation. Blinky pursued, undead and pastel, the blank look in his eyes belying his thirst for death. And then, in an instant, it all changed. Night was day. Light was dark. For the gluttonous refugee had reached his engorged spheroid of power, and just like that, the chaser had become the chasee.

OR

Doom: The Novel

(Excerpt): He turned. He shot. The guy died. He turned again. He shot. Another guy died. He turned slightly. He shot. A guy died. He shot again. A guy died. He turned. He shot. He missed. He shot again. A guy died. He turned. He shot. A guy died. He was shot. He lost a portion of his life force. He shot. A guy died. He shot. A guy died. He moved forward. He turned. He shot. A guy died.

YOU MUST CHOOSE!

Would you rather...

HAVE AN 8 INCH WIDE INNIE BELLY-BUTTON

OR

HAVE A 10 INCH LONG OUTIE BELLY-BUTTON?

Would you rather...

cut off your arm using nothing but mini tweezers

OR

remove all of your teeth using a bottle opener?

Would you rather...

have a Norton virus checker for your body that would notify you about all viruses you get

OR

have a grammar check alert you when you speak incorrectly?

Would you rather...

have been college roommates with Gandhi

OR

Rube Goldberg?

Things to consider: late night BS sessions, elaborate phone answering devices, who was banging more chicks?

YOU MUST CHOOSE!

Would you rather...

have the letters on your keyboard randomly change places every day

OR

only be able to type with your thumbs?

Would you rather...

refer to yourself as "The Commandant"

OR

refer to yourself as "The 'Your Name'" like "The Donald" Trump?

YOU MUST CHOOSE!

Would you rather...

have Tyra Banks's forehead

OR

have Tyra Banks's brain?

Would you rather...

be a shapeshifter who can shift into the likeness of anyone named Darryl

OR

be tripolar (your moods swing wildly from joyful, to depressed, to being convinced you are an NBA referee in the middle of a game)?

YOU MUST CHOOSE!

Authors' Debate

Would you rather...

fart a flamethrower's flame

Flame it Up by David Gomberg

Flamefarter. That's what your superhero name would be, along with the eponymous Marvel comic and mega-blockbuster they make based on your life. How exactly do you plan to fight crime by excreting dry ice? Fecal scented carbon dioxide is not a substantial impediment to villains and criminals. Not in the 21st century. And God, imagine the pain. Dry ice in its solid form is −109.3 °F. Put simply, its enthalpy of sublimation (Hsub) at −78.5 °C (−109.3 °F) is 571 kJ/kg (245 BTU/lb). Ouch!

YOU MUST CHOOSE!

Authors' Debate

OR *defecate dry ice?*

Ice Man by Justin Heimberg

Dumping dry ice will chap the sphincter, true, but farting flames isn't exactly Charmin-soft on the tussy. I think "Flamefarter" may be suffering from delusions of grandeur along with his third degree anus burns. A more logical comic book moniker for the one with the flaming anus is The Human Kiln, seeing that firing pottery via fart is the most utilitarian function I can think of for such a "talent." You'd have to buy crotchless pants or chaps since you'll be singeing your trousers every time a silent-but-wounding whisper of a soft flamefart ekes out. With the dry ice, your rectum will chap up after the first few BM's, and then you're just dealing with smoking stools. Not too shabby.

YOU MUST CHOOSE!

EXTRA EXTREMELY EXTREME EXTRAS:

Would You Rather...? Presents 10 Things to Do at a Job Interview to Screw with the Interviewer

① At the top of your resume, print (in italics) song lyrics that inspire you, such as:

I would fight for you - I'd lie for you
Walk the wire for you - yeah I'd die for you
You know it's true.
Everything I do - I do it for you.
      — Bryan Adams (from *Robin Hood, Prince of Thieves*)

② Smell your fingers periodically.

③ Quote Jesus a little too often.

④ Need a ride home.

⑤ Refer to yourself several times as a "grown-ass man," as in "I don't need micromanaging. I'm a grown-ass man."

⑥ Bring an "attorney" to your interview. Consult the attorney whenever you're asked a question, and have the attorney whisper to you before answering.

YOU MUST CHOOSE!

⑦ Wink frequently.

⑧ Bring a pocket dictionary. Every time the interviewer mentions a mildly sophisticated word, open the dictionary, look up the word, repeat the definition quietly, and then close the dictionary and answer the question normally.

⑨ List all of your references as "Deceased."

⑩ Listen attentively to the interviewer's explanation of the company. Then, with a deadpan expression, point to the appropriate body parts and say "Milk, milk, lemonade, 'round the corner, fudge is made." (Perfect opportunity to wink.)

For more material like this, check out the book *MindF*cks* by Justin Heimberg and David Gomberg and Google the short videos *Do Unto Others*.

YOU MUST CHOOSE!

2

Extremely Sexual

Sex is a perfect example of an area where the boundaries of "extreme" expand every day. S&M is the new second base. Threesomes have given way to dodecasomes. A kiss goodnight on a first date? That's right, it's been replaced with a goodnight Cleveland Steamer on the first date. And so, we as cultural commentators, must "progress" with the times, offering up quandaries that play with the ever-expanding limits of sexual taboo.

Would you rather...

orgasm every 20 years

OR

orgasm every 20 yards?

Things to consider: the hundred yard dash, long hallways, playing football

Would you rather...

come home to find your parents reading your diary

OR

reading the *Kama Sutra*?

Would you rather...

have genitalia that whistle like a tea pot when you get turned on

OR

genitalia that emit a loud buzz and flashes a *Family Feud* "X" when you're turned off?

YOU MUST CHOOSE!

Would you rather have sex with...

Johnny Depp **OR** Brad Pitt?

50 Cent **OR** Dr. Drew?

Matthew Fox **OR** Jake Gyllenhaal?

Jimmy Kimmel **OR** Mitt Romney?

a first cousin of your choice **OR** John Madden?

Would you rather...

have sex with Padma Lakshmi

OR

get a five course *Top Chef* meal cooked to your specifications?

YOU MUST CHOOSE!

Would you rather have sex with...

Angelina Jolie **OR** Megan Fox?

Halle Berry **OR** Heidi Klum?

Reese Witherspoon **OR** Elisabeth Hasselbeck?

George Clooney **OR** Kirstie Alley at her heaviest/sloppiest?

Would you rather...

receive a Twitter tweet every time your partner has sexual thoughts about another person

OR

not?

YOU MUST CHOOSE!

Would you rather...

passionately make out with a heavy drooler

OR

give oral sex to a heavy farter?

Would you rather...

be unable to refrain from spastically "freaking" anyone you see over 70 years old

OR

upon saying goodbye, be unable to refrain from patting anyone under 14 on the butt with a friendly tap and a wink?

Would you rather...

get sexually aroused by the *NBC Nightly News* theme

OR

be turned on by dirty talk spoken in the style of a Cockney British orphan child?

YOU MUST CHOOSE!

Would you rather...

have your sexual fantasies edited for appropriate television viewing

OR

have the *Reading Rainbow* guy appear and tell you the moral at the end of every masturbation fantasy?

Things to consider: passionate kissing, implied intercourse

Would you rather have sex with...

Jessica Simpson if she gained 100 pounds **OR** Helen Mirren?

Jessica Alba and get herpes **OR** Meredith Viera and get a new X-box?

a limbless Adriana Lima **OR** Joy Behar?

Would you rather have sex with...

Brad Pitt if he gained 60 pounds all in the gut **OR** Jonah Hill?

a gap-toothed Matt Damon **OR** Chris Parnell?

Dr. Phil **OR** a racist-remark-spouting Tom Brady?

YOU MUST CHOOSE!

Would you rather...

have the sounds of your love-making uploaded everyday on iTunes

OR

have a video of you in the throes of masturbation posted on YouTube?

Would you rather...

have upside-down genitals

OR

have genitals rotated 90 degrees?

Would you rather...

have your wedding videographer be Joe Francis (creator of *Girls Gone Wild*)

OR

have your wedding ceremony officiated by Flavor Flav?

YOU MUST CHOOSE!

Would you rather...

have "innie" nipples

OR

inch-long curly nipples?

Would you rather...

have a sexual partner who has a lettuce fetish

OR

a foot-measuring device fetish?

Would you rather...

have sex with Cookie Monster

OR

Oscar the Grouch

Things to consider: CM's insatiable and feverish dining style, bad boys, stench

YOU MUST CHOOSE!

Would you rather have sex with...

Natalie Portman **OR** Mila Kunis?

Kate Hudson **OR** Anne Hathaway?

Hayden Panettiere **OR** Mandy Moore?

Christina Ricci **OR** Scarlett Johansson?

Dame Judi Dench **OR** Chyna?

Would you rather...

have sex on a sex swing

OR

in zero gravity?

YOU MUST CHOOSE!

Would you rather have sex with...

Javier Bardem **OR** Christian Bale?

Jon Stewart **OR** Stephen Colbert?

Adam Brody **OR** Michael Cera?

Nick Carter **OR** Aaron Carter?

a Transformer **OR** Mike Huckabee?

Would you rather...

be a teenager in the free love '60s

OR

in the '70s when air-brushed vans with beds and shag carpets were totally acceptable?

YOU MUST CHOOSE!

Would you rather be forced to always have sex...

to the soundtrack of *High School Musical* **OR** festive Indian music?

in strobe light **OR** with NASCAR airing in the background?

in libraries **OR** in janitorial closets?

Would you rather have all of your sexual dreams directed by...

Jerry Bruckheimer **OR** Judd Apatow?

the Wachowski brothers **OR** the Coen brothers?

David Lynch **OR** Pixar?

YOU MUST CHOOSE!

Would you rather...

orgasm every time your cell phone rings

OR

have your cell phone ring every time you are about to orgasm?

Would you rather...

always have sex standing up

OR

without ever facing one another?

Would you rather...

(men read as "date someone with...")
have no vagina

OR

have 17 vaginas all over your body?

YOU MUST CHOOSE!

Would you rather...

have a partner have to pee in the middle of sex

OR

answer a text message in the middle of sex?

Would you rather...

relive your first kiss

OR

relive your first sexual experience?

Would you rather...

spank

OR

be spanked?

YOU MUST CHOOSE!

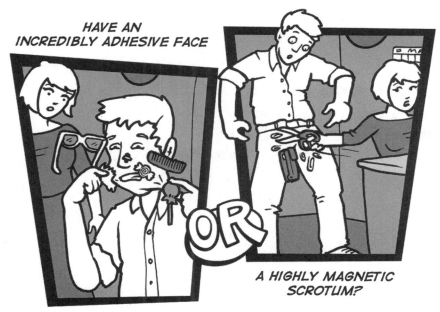

Would you rather...

HAVE AN INCREDIBLY ADHESIVE FACE

OR

A HIGHLY MAGNETIC SCROTUM?

EXTREMELY SEXUAL

41

Would you rather change your name to...

(women, read as "marry and take the name of")

Derrick Fingerblast

OR

Ronald Queefcloud?

Would you rather...

be able to blow visible kisses across a room

OR

be able to fart directionally with an accuracy of 40 feet?

YOU MUST CHOOSE!

Would you ever have sex...

in a dressing room stall at the mall?

in a car in a public parking lot?

in your parents' bed?

on an airplane?

in the windmill of a minigolf course at night 'cause you think no one is there but then someone comes out, and you quickly try to pretend you are playing golf, but you have no clubs and your pants are around your ankles, so you just look like some kind of mime performance art group and you get arrested and have to pay a fine and are banned from that Putt-Putt forever?

YOU MUST CHOOSE!

Would you rather...

have a three-way with Carrie Underwood and Clay Aiken **OR** Adam Lambert and Kelly Clarkson?

Sarah Palin and John McCain **OR** Barack Obama and Hillary Clinton?

Serena Williams and Venus Williams **OR** Petra Nemcová and McLovin (in character)?

Would you rather...

have a threesome with Heidi and Spencer
OR
a brawl with Heidi and Spencer?

YOU MUST CHOOSE!

Would you...

make an agreement with your partner to allow each other three celebrities with whom infidelity would be permitted? If so, who would each of you pick?

Would you rather...

have sex with all celebrities whose last names begin with L **OR** W?

G **OR** D?

C **OR** R?

Would you rather...

come home to find your partner cheating on you

OR

wake up in the middle of the night to find your partner online and masturbating to screen shots of Fozzie Bear?

YOU MUST CHOOSE!

Would you rather...

have feathered hair

OR

have feathered pubic hair?

Would you rather...

have sex with the man who voices AOL

OR

with the man who voices movie previews?

Would you rather...

receive the memories of anyone you sleep with

OR

not?

YOU MUST CHOOSE!

Would you rather have...

(women read as "have a partner with...")
a set of drill-bit like different penis heads

OR

a penis that can be adjusted and reconfigured like a pipe cleaner?

Would you rather have sex with...

Amanda Bynes **OR** Hilary Duff?

Michelle Pfeiffer **OR** Heather Locklear?

Sarah Jessica Parker **OR** Meg Ryan?

Jessica Biel **OR** Cameron Diaz?

Perez Hilton **OR** Tim Gunn?

YOU MUST CHOOSE!

Would you rather have sex with...

The Rock **OR** Denzel Washington?

Bono **OR** Sting?

Ryan Gosling **OR** Jake Gyllenhaal?

Justin Timberlake **OR** Kanye West?

John Mayer **OR** Jack Johnson?

Would you rather...

know what it is like to physically experience sex as the opposite gender

OR

know what it is like to emotionally experience love as the opposite gender?

YOU MUST CHOOSE!

Would you rather...

have nipples that turn green and burst out of your clothing when you get angry

OR

have grappling hook nipples?

Would you rather...

have breast implants filled with birdseed

OR

breast implants filled with the stuff in rainsticks?

Would you rather...

have a total poker face when having an orgasm

OR

speak like an old radio crooner during sex?

YOU MUST CHOOSE!

Authors' Debate

Would you rather...

your only porn be science books

Science Books – David Gomberg

I'll take the vague shape of the body, organs exposed, over the history book masturbance of a sickly malnourished native Amazonian tribeswoman with diseased saggy breasts dripping to the ground, nipples scraping and tilling the soil. The circulatory system? Hot. Or maybe the pancreas is your thing. One last point: Don't forget that health and sex ed find their way into science books, too. So you can informatively grunt, "I'm gonna ram that labia majoris with the glans of the phallus until I ejaculate my spermatozoa cells!" That's as hot as the specific heat of mercury!

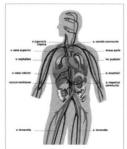

YOU MUST CHOOSE!

OR history books?

History Books – Justin Heimberg

Like you haven't pleasured yourself to Harriet Tubman already? Givin' her the old "Underground Railroad." And Susan B "Doin' it" Anthony? She's got an ass that won't quit. Not until women's suffrage is achieved, at least. (By the way, can we change the word "suffrage" to mean something bad? It's confusing.) The point is that there are plenty of historic vixens to smack it to. The tomboy thing that Joan of Arc has going. The erotic mystique of Cleopatra, the eloquent dirty talk of Abigail Adams. It's true what they say: Sometimes we have to look backward to spew forth.

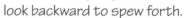

YOU MUST CHOOSE!

EXTRA EXTREMELY EXTREME EXTRAS:
Facts That Sound For a Second Like They Might Be True But Aren't

A small amount of heroin is used in the manufacturing of Sunny Delight Citrus Drink.

Women originally wore makeup for warmth.

The reason Tom Selleck grew his mustache is because it helps with his allergies.

Soccer was invented on pirate ships as a means of cleaning the deck.

Water on the left side of the pool is always colder than water on the right side.

The Chinese government removes organs from Olympic gymnasts and wrestlers to make them lighter.

The back of a stamp has 70% of the daily requirement of riboflavin.

YOU MUST CHOOSE!

Statistically speaking, billiards is America's deadliest sport.

The people in pictures that come with wallets are prisoners whose services are not paid for, but rather mandated by law.

The letter "w" was added to the English language in 1954.

In any room of 20 people, there is a 50% chance that at least two people received the same birthday present last year.

Waffles have indentations on them because on Hanukah, the fleeing Jewish people did not have enough batter to make them to even thickness.

YOU MUST CHOOSE!

Extremely Painful and Extremely Fatal

Feeling a wee bit masochistic, are we? It's ok. It's a part of human nature to have occasional thoughts of self-harm. Of course, the following thoughts are beyond the natural. Did someone say "extreme"?! No? Oh, I thought I heard something. My bad. Anyway, here are some cruel and unusual options to grimace to as you make your choice. And as always, you must choose. *To the extreme!!!!*

Would you rather...

use the "Rabbit" corkscrew to pluck out your left eyeball

OR

have your fingernails and toenails chiseled off one by one?

Would you rather...

have a pebble sewn into the bottom of your left foot

OR

have a sesame seed lodged uncomfortably and permanently between your front teeth?

Would you rather...

take a power drill up each nostril and then snort cayenne pepper

OR

have your testicles used as a pro boxer's speed bag for two minutes?

YOU MUST CHOOSE!

Would you rather...

die a quick death

OR

die an elaborate and drawn-out death by an overly complicated mechanism with a long speech by a James Bond-esque villain?

Would you rather...

be buried alive in a coffin full of fire ants

OR

be buried alive in a coffin with a wacky morning DJ show being piped in?

Would you rather...

have your lips belt-sanded off

OR

your jaw squeezed in a vice until it was dislocated?

YOU MUST CHOOSE!

Would you rather...

be murdered by Carrot Top who performs prop comedy with your dismembered body parts and organs

OR

be murdered by the author of *Family Circus* who offers barely amusing observations about everyday life as he butchers you?

Would you rather...

after you die, be pickled and displayed at the local bar

OR

be frozen in carbonate á la Han Solo and have your model mass-produced and sold as a coffee table at IKEA?

5th Grade Special

Would you rather...

get Indian-burned to death

OR

noogied to death?

YOU MUST CHOOSE!

Would you rather...

swallow and pass a shoehorn

OR

a Rubik's Cube?

Would you rather...

have your face repeatedly paddled for five minutes by ping pong world champions

OR

have somebody do the "got your nose" trick and really rip off your nose in a bloody mess?

Would you rather...

be strangled to death with black licorice

OR

be suffocated by basil leaves?

Things to consider: Novel idea: *The Herb Killer*, he killed leaving nothing but a pleasant scent.

YOU MUST CHOOSE!

Would you rather...

have two ice picks jammed in your ears and then smashed with a mallet

OR

have your arms folded behind your back and forced up until your shoulders popped out of their sockets?

Would you rather fight to the death...

Bambi **OR** Dumbo?

5,000 origami creations **OR** 100 pairs of high-tops?

a supervillain called "The Caddy" **OR** a supervillain called "The Receptionist"?

YOU MUST CHOOSE!

Would you rather...

take a sledgehammer to the back of both your ankles

OR

have your tongue whipped 500 times with a bamboo rod?

Would you rather...

be stoned to death with Koosh balls **OR** with hardboiled eggs?

by light bulbs **OR** cantaloupes?

by Randy Johnson **OR** by Randy Jackson?
Things to consider: Are you better off facing someone with good aim/speed?

Would you rather...

be clobbered to death with zucchini

OR

be suffocated to death with zucchini?

YOU MUST CHOOSE!

Would you rather...

take wire cutters and snip between your fingers centimeter by centimeter all the way to your wrist

OR

take some hedge clippers and clip your ears off?

Would you rather...

insert dozens of popcorn kernels way up into your sinus cavities and then hold your face over heat until the kernels popped

OR

place a lit M80 firecracker in your mouth and hold your breath until it explodes?

Would you rather...

get stuck on an elevator with gossipy seventh grade girls

OR

an Armenian businessman talking loudly on his cell phone?

YOU MUST CHOOSE!

Would you rather...

FIGHT 1 VICIOUS WEREWOLF

OR

8 BASHFUL VAMPIRES?

Would you rather...

get stuck on a desert island with a hot person who you can't have sex with

OR

a hideous person that wants to constantly have sex?

Would you rather...

be killed by a firing squad of badminton birdies

OR

be slapped to death by your entire neighborhood?

Would you rather...

be drawn and quartered

OR

be drawn and fifthed? Sixthed?

YOU MUST CHOOSE!

Would you rather...

sit on a fire hose for five minutes

OR

sit on an electric burner for one minute?

Would you rather...

have an electric tire pump shoot air into both your nostrils at full speed until your nose explodes

OR

have a high-powered vacuum attached to your crotch until at least something separated from your body?

YOU MUST CHOOSE!

Would you rather...

take ten clean shots in the chin from a boxer

OR

have your testicles neatly placed on a tee and then whacked by Tiger Woods?

Would you rather...

be rolling pinned to death

OR

beaten to death with spatulas?

YOU MUST CHOOSE!

Would you rather...

die by car accident

OR

via purple nurple?

Would you rather...

cut your own leg off

OR

cut off your significant other's?

YOU MUST CHOOSE!

Would you rather...

lie spread eagle and have a monster truck run over you right down the middle of your body

OR

be shaken to death in a giant version of Boggle?

Things to consider: imprints on your corpse

Would you rather...

die like a slug (be salted to death)

OR

be lemon-peppered to death? Paprika'ed to death?

Would you rather...

have all your skin peeled off with a carrot peeler

OR

have your arm veins pulled out of your skin by pliers?

YOU MUST CHOOSE!

Pick your trauma.

Would you rather...

be partially molested by a Yeti (groping, improper talk)

OR

be fully molested by Snuggles the Fabric Softener Bear?

Would you rather...

eat thirty jalapeños with no water

OR

use poison ivy to blow your nose?

YOU MUST CHOOSE!

Would you rather...

be fully awake with no painkillers during a liver transplant

OR

during the removal of a testicle?

Would you rather...

get gored by a bull

OR

bullied by a Gore?

Would you rather...

get a paper cut between each of your toes and then step into a bucket of salt

OR

shave with a butcher's knife and then use vinegar aftershave?

YOU MUST CHOOSE!

Death by Chef

Would you rather...

be roasted on a spit until your meat fell off the bone **OR**
be toasted to death?

be butterflied and stuffed with crabmeat and sautéed **OR**
be blended and consumed as a smoothie?

be dehydrated to death **OR** garnished to death?

for ten minutes, dip your foot into a blender set on the lowest setting
OR set on the highest setting?

Would you rather...

be caught in a hailstorm of thumbtacks
OR
a rainstorm of fire-crackers?

YOU MUST CHOOSE!

Would you rather...

set your foot on a tee and have Albert Pujols take a clean swing at it

OR

take a Johan Santana fastball to the small of the back?

Would you rather...

be dipped in liquid nitrogen and then pushed off a ten story building so you shattered upon impact

OR

be fly-swatted to death?

YOU MUST CHOOSE!

Perpetual feelings

Would you rather...

perpetually experience déjà vu **OR** perpetually be about to remember the name of an obscure song but not quite have it?

perpetually have a "turtle" ebbing in and out of your butt **OR** perpetually feel like you do when your chair is about to fall backwards?

perpetually feel the awkwardness of when they sing "Happy Birthday" to you at a restaurant **OR** perpetually feel the lack of enthusiasm and insincerity that one of the singers feels?

YOU MUST CHOOSE!

Water Wars

Would you rather fight to the death...

three manatees **OR** 300 flounder?

20,000 guppies **OR** one swordfish?

five beavers **OR** one retarded merman?

Would you rather...

be strapped to a table and have a drop of water repeatedly drip on your forehead

OR

be strapped to a table and have your eyes continuously pried open as you watch a one week marathon of *According to Jim*?

YOU MUST CHOOSE!

Would you rather...

be submerged into a deep fryer over and over until you died

OR

be microwaved to death?

Would you rather...

melon-ball your tonsils out

OR

punch yourself in the face until you knocked out all of your teeth?

Would you rather...

pull out all of your hair with your bare hands

OR

use a nutcracker on your testicles?

YOU MUST CHOOSE!

Would you rather...

have string tightened throughout your body turning you into a human sausage until the blocked blood flow kills you

OR

be stabbed to death by Capri Sun straws?

Would you rather...

wash your face with liquid nitrogen

OR

floss with razor wire?

YOU MUST CHOOSE!

Authors' Debate

Would you rather fight to the death...

three 90 year-olds

90s Rule – Justin Heimberg

90 year-olds are brittle. Their old bones break and snap like balsa wood. Three year-olds are rubbery, resilient. They bounce back from things. Sure, they'll cry, but in their tantrum, they are that much more dangerous (and annoying.) It's their battle cry. 90 year-olds are most likely nearly blind. There's a decent chance you can turn them on each other by removing their bifocals and capitalizing on their senility. Three year-olds are right at crotch level, which is very dangerous. That's 18 tiny fists to the groin. I don't like those odds.

YOU MUST CHOOSE!

OR 9 three year-olds?

3rd time's the charm – David Gomberg

90 year-olds have hunched up a bit, but they are still roughly full-size. With the nine three year-olds, you can pretty much defend yourself with your legs. A couple of well-reasoned knees to the faces, and those three year-olds will be nursing bloody noses in the corner. 90 year-olds don't give up. They have nothing to lose. They'll scratch, claw, and sink their dentures into you. They'll fight until the last drop of blood drips from their almost empty tank. Three year-olds can be easily distracted. Hand them a Tickle Me Elmo and as they lose themselves in amusement, BAM! – elbow to the jaw.

EXTREMELY PAINFUL AND EXTREMELY FATAL

YOU MUST CHOOSE!

Extra Extremely Extreme extras:
Terrible First Sentences for a Novel

Klarence liked his women like he liked his kickball pitches—slow and smooth.

Barney stood proudly in his lemon-peel pants.

She was all ligaments.

The pilgrim's orgy was a disaster.

Before going in, Larry put his underpants over his fist.

Elegar the Druid plunged his +5 Doom Broad Sword (transferring) into the barked neck of Lezzen the Orc Prince, Shelby the Bloated watching from the dark pools molting like there was no tomorrow.

Needledorf was his name; Needledorf, by coincidence, was also his game.

The joy in his heart spread like athlete's foot (spreads).

The sun set downward.

YOU MUST CHOOSE!

CHAPTER FOUR

Fairly Extreme

This chapter is beyond slightly extreme, more out there than somewhat extreme! That's right, we're talking "Fairly Extreme!"

Would you rather...

have to sit in a baby-seat high chair at all restaurants

OR

have to use a sippy cup for all beverage consumption?
Things to consider: business lunches

Would you rather...

have the National Anthem changed to Chumbawamba's "Tubthumping"

OR

the Pledge of Allegiance changed to the lyrics of "Baby Got Back"?
Things to consider: Place your hand over your heart and try both

Would you rather...

have the pathetic "whah, whah, whah, whah" sound play whenever
something bad happens to you

OR

have the joyful "Price is Right" music play when something
good happens?

YOU MUST CHOOSE!

Would you rather...

the afterlife was a Staples office supply store

OR

an endless corporate retreat?

Would you rather...

have pubic hair eyelashes

OR

have no eyelashes?
Things to consider: mascara

Would you rather...

always look bruised as if beaten but feel no actual pain

OR

feel like you're bruised but look fine?

YOU MUST CHOOSE!

Would you rather...

have rosemary facial hair

OR

compulsively greet people with a "healing" palm to the forehead and accompanying praise to the Lord?

Would you rather...

have a wedding in the tone of a screwball comedy

OR

a Kung Fu movie?

Things to consider: ice sculptures, bouquet battles, ninja veils

YOU MUST CHOOSE!

Inventoids by Merle Pelsborp

Which coffee invention would you rather have?

a coffee straw that cools coffee enough that you don't burn your mouth

OR

a sugar dispenser that dispenses an exact spoonful of sugar with each tap?

Would you rather eat all meals...

with chopsticks **OR** with a spork?

with your hands **OR** by being fed by other people?

with Big Bird **OR** with Lauren Conrad?

YOU MUST CHOOSE!

Would you rather...

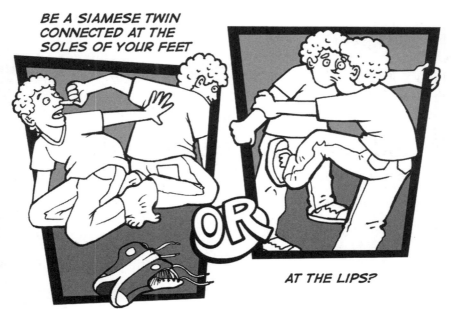

BE A SIAMESE TWIN CONNECTED AT THE SOLES OF YOUR FEET

OR

AT THE LIPS?

Would you...

tackle an 80 year-old for no reason for $1,000 bucks? If you got $1,000 for every 80+ year-old you tackled in a day, how many would you go for? How would you spend the day?

Would you...

get a tattoo on every square inch of your body for two million dollars and then get it laser-removed for another two million?

Would you...

tattoo a $ sign on your scrotum for $50,000?

YOU MUST CHOOSE!

Would you rather...

your doctor spoke in Seuss rhymes...

You have six months to live:

Your heart is a pumping

Your heart is a popping

But one year in half

Your heart will be stopping

It'll clonk, it'll clank

It'll cloink, it'll clunk

And then your body will fall

Just like that – kerplunk!

And you'll be tossed in the ground

With all sorts of junk.

YOU MUST CHOOSE!

OR your boss spoke in Seuss rhymes…

You're fired.

Clean out your in-box

And jump in your out-box

Wipe clear your desk

And forget all your stox

They've been locked away

With ten thousand lox

And just for good measure

An arctic snow fox

So goodbye and sorry

If you feel disgraced

That you and three others have all been replaced

By a 16 year-old with spots on his face.

YOU MUST CHOOSE!

Would you rather...

HAVE PERMANENTLY LATHERED HAIR

OR

ONLY BE ABLE TO MOVE AROUND BY MOON-WALKING?

Would you rather...

have a speech impediment where you switch "s" and "t" sounds

OR

"p" and "w" sounds?

Things to consider: "pow-wows"; "popcorn"; "suck my tits"

Would you rather...

get facial hair on the upper half of your face

OR

have webbed thighs?

Would you rather...

recite famous historical speeches in your sleep

OR

reenact '80s sitcoms dialogue?

YOU MUST CHOOSE!

Would you rather...

when upset, always and exclusively exclaim "Consarnit"

OR

always mutter a low, long, rumbling "Sheeeeeeeyiiiiiiiiittttttttttt"?

Would you rather your last words be written...

by Shakespeare **OR** Dr. Seuss?

by Martin Luther King **OR** Louis C.K.?

by Jesus **OR** Three 6 Mafia? Jeff Foxworthy?

Would you rather...

walk like an Egyptian

OR

walk nothing like an Egyptian, with no resemblance whatsoever in gait, stride, or posture?

YOU MUST CHOOSE!

Would you rather have your legal name be...

Balls Johnson **OR** Stubby McGraw?

Titty Watson **OR** Jackie Taint?

Fritz Nutchap Analbags **OR** Lars Scrotie-scrote Asspacket?
Things to consider: This question paraphrased from Shakespeare's *The Tempest*

Would you rather have the exact same handwriting as...

Michael Vick **OR** Joe Biden?

Kurt Cobain **OR** Leonardo da Vinci?
Things to consider: forging journals

YOU MUST CHOOSE!

Would you rather...

the upper half of your face be unable to move

OR

the left half?

Would you rather...

have a hunchback

OR

a hunchfront?

Would you rather...

have Vulcan ears

OR

a Vulcan personality?

YOU MUST CHOOSE!

Would you rather...

have an asshole for a shadow

OR

have an echo with a Canadian accent?

Would you rather...

always be bobbing and weaving like a boxer

OR

have your at-rest position be the Running Man dance?

Would you rather...

get stuck on an elevator with sweaty vaguely foreign guys

OR

DJs who want to talk incessantly about their "fat beats"?

YOU MUST CHOOSE!

Would you rather...

have whatever you are thinking Twittered to your parents
every two minutes

OR

receive a Twitter with whatever your parents are thinking?

Would you rather...

be a world class sprinter but only when fully erect

OR

be a world class swimmer but only while naked?
Things to consider: pelvic thrusting at the finish line

YOU MUST CHOOSE!

If on Jeopardy, would you rather use as your question format...

"Is that a _____ in your pants or are you just happy to see me?"

OR

"You want me to say _____ , don't you?"

"Should I kick your face in, Alex, or is it _____ ?"

OR

"How 'bout a little bit of _____ ?"

YOU MUST CHOOSE!

Would you rather your child join...

a theater troupe **OR** the baseball team?

the D&D club **OR** choir?

a cooking class **OR** the Boy Scouts?

Things to consider: The Boy Scouts have made their position on homosexuality clear. A 1991 Position Statement states: "We believe that homosexual conduct is inconsistent with the requirement in the Scout Oath that a Scout be morally straight and in the Scout Law that a Scout be clean in word and deed, and that homosexuals do not provide a desirable role model for Scouts." That's right, God forbid any gay people get in the way of the manly Boy Scouts as they bedeck themselves in ascots and earn patches for craftwork to be sewn on their green felt sashes. If you're gonna act gay, accept gays. Next caller.

Would you rather have Dick Cheney's...

literal heart

OR

figurative heart?

YOU MUST CHOOSE!

Would you rather...

conduct all conversation with your partner in the tone of local newscast banter

OR

in the tone of a morning zoo show?

Things to consider: sound effects, wacky guests, "That's great Sheila. (Chuckle) Now turning our attention to the children…"

Would you rather...

be blow-dried to death

OR

slow-baked to death on a tanning bed?

Things to consider: corpse appearance for funeral

YOU MUST CHOOSE!

Would you rather...

suffer from ingrown eyelashes

OR

eyeball warts?

Would you rather...

upon making any mistake, have someone appear who always sarcastically slow-claps to rub it in

OR

be unable to drink a beverage without doing a spit take on the first sip?

Things to consider: state dinners, wedding toasts, first dates

YOU MUST CHOOSE!

Would you rather...

emit the sound of nails on a blackboard whenever you scratch an itch

OR

cry like a three year-old when something doesn't go your way?

Would you rather...

slide under your covers, only to discover a dozen roaches scurrying about

OR

sit on the toilet, only to discover a rat swimming around?

Would you rather...

use a power drill as a Q-Tip

OR

get a lower back tattoo with lemon juice?

YOU MUST CHOOSE!

Would you rather...

get a Superglue facial

OR

use Superglue as a sexual lubricant?

Would you rather...

have a navel with a Magic 8-Ball readout in it

OR

have barbecue sauce saliva?

Things to consider: combining belly-dancing with fortune-telling, ribs

Would you rather...

bite into a popsicle with your front teeth 50 times

OR

get a paper cut on your eye?

YOU MUST CHOOSE!

Would you rather...

always look like you're severely constipated

OR

always be miming trying to keep a basketball spinning on your finger?

Would you rather...

grow an extra one inch layer of flesh for every year of your life like a tree grows wood

OR

shed your skin and hair every autumn?

Would you rather...

consume a mouse smoothie

OR

a tarantula wrap?

YOU MUST CHOOSE!

Would you rather...

have your nipples dipped in liquid nitrogen and shattered

OR

your earlobes clipped off with garden hedgers?

Would you rather...

eat Squirrel Intestine Alfredo

OR

a Bull Testicle Parmigiana sandwich?

Would you rather...

have Meg Ryan's cosmetic surgeon

OR

Tom Cruise's spiritual advisor?

YOU MUST CHOOSE!

Would you rather...

dive through a Slip-N-Slide covered in sheep excrement and urine

OR

get a Mentos and Diet Coke enema?

Would you rather...

speak like a wise Native American chief whenever you're chilly

OR

sprout facial hair at the first sign of traffic, with it getting worse as road congestion does?

Would you rather...

have the arm waddle of the world's fattest woman

OR

have the varicose leg veins of the world's oldest woman?

Things to consider: possible flight?

YOU MUST CHOOSE!

Would you rather...

invariably get stuck behind someone at least a foot taller than you at every movie, concert, play, etc.

OR

invariably get stuck behind Slowface Johnson whenever you need to get somewhere fast on the street, at an airport, etc.?

Would you rather...

have a perpetual watch glint shining in your eyes

OR

be compelled to whistle "Camptown Races" whenever seeing something purple?

Would you rather...

have literal crow's feet around your eyes

OR

have Chuck Woolery photoshopped into all of your wedding photos?

YOU MUST CHOOSE!

Which Blues song would you rather hear...

"I Didn't Get into Harvard (But I Did Get into Brown, my Safety School)"

OR

"Grass Stains Ain't Coming Out"?

Would you rather...

take your measurements 34-28-35 (for example) and have them randomly mixed up

OR

gain 5 pounds in one random place on your body?

Would you rather...

have a type of Tourette's Syndrome that causes you to exclaim "Yeah, Boyeeee!" every twenty minutes

OR

that causes you to exclaim "Here, diagonally!"?

YOU MUST CHOOSE!

Would you rather...

have to make your Number 2s in the shower

OR

in mail slots?

Would you rather...

bitch slap a polar bear

OR

spit in the eye of a tiger?

YOU MUST CHOOSE!

Would you rather...

have cankles (no distinction between your calves and ankles)

OR

a nin (no distinction between your neck and chin)?

Would you rather permanently speak...

'70s jive

OR

CSI: Miamese (a language based on David Caruso's wry comments and bad puns)?

Things to consider: "Up top, Blood!"; "It's about time this garbage man... gets recycled."

YOU MUST CHOOSE!

Authors' Debate

Would you rather...

your genitalia was located on the palm of your hand

Neck – Justin Heimberg

One word. Ascot. It can just be kind of your thing. With neckitals®, you can combine the ecstasy of eating with the ecstasy of sex—if you swallow just right, applying gentle pressure to the underside of the neck, you can stimulate your g-spot. If your junk was on your hands, be you a woman or man, you'd have to always explain why you are wearing that one mitten and why you aren't applauding after a show; or worse, you will applaud, hurting or arousing yourself with each clap until your mitten gets soiled. Plus, through rigorous sex, one of your arms would become way more muscular than the other, making you grotesquely asymmetrical (as if having hand genitals wasn't bad enough).

YOU MUST CHOOSE!

OR the front of your neck?

Hand it over – David Gomberg

Imagine sex. On your hand, you have all kinds of maneuverability. With neck-nuts, you're relegated to lying down and letting someone ride or thrust against you until you can't breathe. And yes, you can hide your hand genitals with a mitten and learn to write with the other hand. But neck balls, those are tough to hide (as is neck labia.) In fact being a woman is particularly distasteful in that with each intercourse thrust, you're getting a mouthful of mantuft™. And you won't develop asymmetrical muscles, because, on one hand (literally), you have the goods to have sex with; and on the other hand, literally sort of, you'd be using it to stimulate yourself during self-pleasure. Yin and yang. The balance of life.

YOU MUST CHOOSE!

EXTRA EXTREMELY EXTREME EXTRAS:
Read this page if stoned.

Flounder Flounder Flounder Flounder Flounder Flounder Flounder
Flounder Flounder Flounder Flounder Flounder Flounder Flounder
Flounder Flounder Flounder Flounder Flounder Flounder Flounder
Flounder Flounder Flounder Flounder Flounder Flounder Flounder
Flounder Flounder Flounder Flounder Flounder Flounder Flounder
Flounder Flounder Flounder Flounder Flounder Flounder Flounder
Flounder Flounder Flounder Flounder Flounder Flounder Flounder
Flounder Flounder Flounder Flounder Flounder Flounder Flounder
Flounder Flounder Flounder Flounder Flounder Flounder Flounder
Flounder Flounder Flounder Flounder Flounder Flounder Flounder
Flounder Flounder Flounder Flounder Flounder Flounder Flounder
Flounder Flounder Flounder Flounder Flounder Flounder Flounder
Flounder Flounder Flounder Flounder Flounder Flounder Flounder
Flounder Flounder Flounder Flounder Flounder Phlounder Flounder
Flounder Flounder Flounder Flounder Flounder Flounder Flounder
Flounder Flounder Flounder Flounder Flounder Flounder Flounder
Flounder Flounder Flounder Flounder Flounder Flounder Flounder
Flounder Flounder Flounder Flounder Flounder Flounder Flounder
Flounder Flounder Flounder Flounder Flounder Flounder Flounder
Flounder Flounder Flounder Flounder Flounder Flounder Flounder
Flounder Flounder Flounder Flounder Flounder Flounder Flounder

Would you rather...

ONLY BE ABLE TO
EAT ORANGE FOODS

OR

ONLY BE ABLE TO EAT FOOD
STARTING WITH THE LETTER "K"?

Extremely Gross
and Extremely Embarrassing

Pain is one thing, but the nausea of a gross undertaking or the emotional agony of an embarrassing situation can be even worse. To the extreme! Damn it, that didn't quite work. We've got to get the hang of this "to the extreme" thing, eventually. Jeez. Anyway, take a dive into the downright disgusting mixed with the awful and awkward... to the... never mind.

Would you rather...

eat a jelly doughnut full of snot

OR

a danish iced with yak semen?

Would you rather...

your photo was used on a herpes medication billboard

OR

for an ad for a gay dating site?

Would you rather...

have masturbated to Internet porn only to realize you left on the Skype video conference with your mom

OR

find out all of your drunk dials have been recorded and posted on iTunes?

YOU MUST CHOOSE!

Would you rather...

throw up in zero gravity

OR

have to unclog a toilet with your bare hands?

Would you rather...

consume a sundae of pig stomach dolloped with hot vomit sprinkled with mice droppings topped with the testicle of a gnu

OR

a drink a grande fecesccino?

Would you rather...

watch your grandparents' sloppy make-out/grope session

OR

discover they are watching yours lasciviously?

YOU MUST CHOOSE!

Would you rather...

brush your teeth nightly for six months with a copious inch-long portion of smegma

OR

change your name to Smegma?

Would you rather...

French kiss someone four times your age

OR

French kiss a goat?

Would you rather...

bathe in a tub of maggots

OR

fat drained from liposuction patients?

YOU MUST CHOOSE!

Would you rather...

have to wear clothes taken daily from _____ 's
dirty hamper

(insert least hygienic acquaintance)

OR

sleep each night in a bed recently "occupied" by_____ ?

(insert most sexually deviant friend)

Would you rather...

give a drunken wedding toast at your sibling's wedding where you keep
talking about how hot her friends are

OR

witness and cringe to a wedding toast from your dad that has
numerous sexual stories and graphic sexual imagery?

Would you rather...

have to milk a cow with your mouth until a bucket is full

OR

do the same by squeezing your butt cheeks?

YOU MUST CHOOSE!

Would you rather...

have a plate of human skin Carpaccio

OR

drink a glass of aged room temperature anal sweat?

Would you rather...

vomit on the floor while letting loose with diarrhea in the toilet

OR

let loose with diarrhea on the floor while vomiting in the toilet?

Things to consider: Question excerpted from Descartes' *Discourse on Method, Meditations on First Philosophy*

Would you rather...

let a cockroach crawl in your mouth and down your throat

OR

up your nose and out the other nostril?

YOU MUST CHOOSE!

Would you rather...

eat four scoops of hair from a barber shop floor and then cough up a cigar-shaped hairball like a cat

OR

eat a regurgitated cat hairball?

Would you rather...

swallow battery acid and pass it through your bladder and urethra Franklin

OR

eat several throwing stars and pass them all the way through your digestive system through your rectum?

Would you rather...

eat a soft serve cone of dog feces

OR

"Shake and Bake" litter-encrusted cat dung?

YOU MUST CHOOSE!

Would you rather...

use used Kleenex to wipe your ass

OR

use used toilet paper to blow your nose?

Would you rather...

lick a camel's anus

OR

hand-clean the dingleberries of a grumpy St. Bernard? An irritable donkey? Michael Moore?

YOU MUST CHOOSE!

Would you rather...

do a shot of bull semen

OR

taste a spoonful of horse afterbirth?

Would you rather...

wring out ten maxipads straight into your mouth

OR

receive a fire hose enema?

Would you rather...

go to a dentist with Parkinson's

OR

a proctologist with Parkinson's?

YOU MUST CHOOSE!

Would you rather...

be caught masturbating by your grandfather

OR

vice-versa? Grandmother? the ghost of Thomas Jefferson?

Would you rather eat ice cream flavored...

Salmon Chunk **OR** Bubble Gum (with already chewed wads)

Broccoli Sorbet **OR** Dirty Coins N' Cream?

Post Nasal Drip Swirl **OR** Roadkill Fudge?

Newsprint **OR** Ku Klux Kreme?

YOU MUST CHOOSE!

Would you rather...

kiss your grandmother goodbye, only to have her slip you the tongue

OR

bite into a turkey kielbasa, only to discover veins?

Would you rather...

have to eat like a baby bird where your mom regurgitates partially digested food into your mouth

OR

only be able to eat food that has been partially digested and excreted by some living thing?

Would you rather...

find a condom at the bottom of your vanilla milkshake

OR

sip a bowl of gazpacho only to discover a pubic hair at the bottom?

YOU MUST CHOOSE!

Would you rather...

eat a sushi roll of a maggot-encrusted slug

OR

eat a caramel apple rolled on the floor of a barber shop?

Would you rather have a bird crap...

in your hair **OR** on your new car?

in your ear **OR** all over your clothes?

in your eye **OR** in your mouth?

YOU MUST CHOOSE!

EXTRA EXTREMELY EXTREME EXTRAS:
Increasingly Egregious Misspellings Of Hanukah

Hannukah

Chanukaha

Ghananka

Chunkyka

Honkeykah

Donkeykong

YOU MUST CHOOSE!

CHAPTER SIX

Unextreme Powers

Okay, so the truth is that these powers are not necessarily extreme.
They tend to fall a little short of "super" as superpowers go. Nonetheless, will you use these extremely unextreme abilities for good or evil? You, and you alone, must choose... *to the unextreme!*

Would you rather...

be spared the annoyance of magazines' inserted subscription cards

OR

have pinpoint TiVo stopping accuracy?

Would you rather...

poop fragrant potpourri bundles

OR

have permanent Listerine breath?
Things to consider: romance, defecating in crystal bowls

Would you rather...

have an hour-long chat with your 12 year-old self

OR

with your 72 year-old self?

YOU MUST CHOOSE!

Would you rather...

be able to scan documents into your computer with your tongue

OR

be able to weed-whack with your foot?

Would you rather...

have Thomas Dewey (of Decimal System fame) as your personal organizer

OR

George Washington Carver as your personal chef?

Would you rather...

have lemon-flavored hangnails

OR

naturally scab corduroy?

YOU MUST CHOOSE!

Which iPod app would you want...

one that takes a picture of someone and then spits back which celebrity they look most like **OR** a Zagat-like public restroom guide?

one that makes the phone edible **OR** one that emits a blinding ray?

one that makes disco ball lights **OR** iRazor, where you can shave your face with the screen?

iGina **OR** iSoapdispenser?

iLiner **OR** iBrator?

Would you rather...

your dreams were written by Roald Dahl
OR
Judd Apatow?

YOU MUST CHOOSE!

Would you rather...

have self-lathering skin

OR

refrigerated pockets?

Would you rather...

have a yarmulke with razor sharp edges that you use to fight off bad guys like the guy in James Bond's *Goldfinger*

OR

be able to fight and kill with office supplies?

YOU MUST CHOOSE!

Would you rather...

be able to automatically *dictate* your actual mood just by selecting a MySpace emoticon

OR

instantly be doing whatever you change your Facebook status to?

Would you rather...

be able to come in fourth in any race any time

OR

be able to high jump at an Olympic level but only when dressed in the shorts-on-the-outside-of-the-sweatpants look?

YOU MUST CHOOSE!

Would you rather...

be able to control an army of origami creatures

OR

an army of lunch meats?

Would you rather...

be a supervillain called the Grammarian (weapons shaped like punctuation marks, perfectly expressed diabolical speeches, constantly correcting the grammar of your foes)

OR

The Doorman? (weapons include keys and door knobs; always engaging in trivial polite conversation as you kill foes).

YOU MUST CHOOSE!

Would you rather...

have unlimited texting

OR

permission for unlimited farting?

Would you rather...

have a pet Pegasus, but one with a personality that is very "dickish"

OR

have a centaur friend who is constantly shamelessly hitting on you?

Would you rather...

be immune to "order envy"

OR

have "The Yellow Rose of Texas" emanate whenever you urinate?

YOU MUST CHOOSE!

Would you rather...

have your hair grown out and braided into a sensible backpack

OR

have your fingernails cultivated and shaped into lock picks?

Would you rather...

have your peeled dead skin taste like cherry fruit roll-up

OR

have licorice hair?

YOU MUST CHOOSE!

Inventoids by Merle Pelsborp

Would you rather...

have a bed that heats on one side but not the other (to mitigate male-female disparity)

OR

have a "toilet blender" (a garbage disposal for your toilet to prevent clogs)?

Would you rather...

have the ability to swap facial features with friends

OR

have the freedom to swap sexual partners with no emotional or moral fall-out?

YOU MUST CHOOSE!

Would you rather be reincarnated as...

a rabbit **OR** a snake?

a Midwestern farmer **OR** an Ivy League a capella singer?

an average accountant **OR** the next-door neighbor of an "Extreme Home Makeover" recipient?

Would you rather...

have heightened intuition in Rock Paper Scissors

OR

be able to increase the speeds of escalators?

Would you rather...

have a daily allowance of 10,000 calories with no weight gain

OR

have the ability to induce instant and intense diarrhea in anyone you wish?

Things to consider: public debates, dinner parties

YOU MUST CHOOSE!

Would you rather...

be able to personally choose every member of the Supreme Court

OR

every Oscar winner?

Things to consider: Chief Justice Björk

Would you rather...

always appear half your age

OR

3/4 of your weight?

Would you rather...

have a belly button vortex that sucks objects within two inches into nothingness

OR

be a supervillain called the Mime, who can mime objects into existence?

Would you rather...

never miss a shot when playing quarters

OR

have unlimited quarters?

YOU MUST CHOOSE!

Would you rather...

have the freckles on your back form a perfect astrological map

OR

have your pulse beat to the guitar riff of "Sunshine of Your Love"?

Would you rather...

be able to pop popcorn kernels in your closed fist

OR

have your Bluetooth headset snap into your navel?

Would you rather...

tan in the pattern of desert camouflage

OR

have nostrils that dispense mustard and ketchup
when you blow your nose?

Things to consider: military career, what if it were dessert camouflage

YOU MUST CHOOSE!

Would you rather...

be able to Twitter updates straight into subscribers' brains

OR

be able to receive Twitter updates the same way?

Would you rather...

be able to spit tobacco with pinpoint accuracy up to fifty feet

OR

be able to fart to the tune of the opening to any song?

Would you rather...

be able to understand quantum physics

OR

be able to prove via geometrical proof that Baby does indeed got back?

YOU MUST CHOOSE!

Would you rather...

have a pocket in the skin of your thigh

OR

have a working zip-up change purse for a scrotum?
Things to consider: the beach

Would you rather...

have a photographic memory where you remember everything you see

OR

have a phonographic memory where you remember everything you hear with a scratchy slightly high pitched old-timey sound?

Would you rather...

be able to dry yourself without a towel by shaking like a dog

OR

be able to lick your nuts like said dog?

YOU MUST CHOOSE!

Would you rather...

be able to perform electrolysis with your finger tips

OR

be able to type your thoughts by resting your head on your computer keyboard?

Would you rather...

have a thumb that dispenses moisturizer

OR

have nipples that can act as cigarette lighters?

Would you rather...

have eyes that can change color to best match your outfit

OR

be able to change your race on command?

YOU MUST CHOOSE!

Would you rather...

be able to shake off unwanted hair like a wet dog

OR

be able to reposition fat cells like squeezing a tube of toothpaste?

Would you rather...

(Men read as have a partner with...)
have a naturally Brazilian butt

OR

a naturally Brazilian wax job?

Would you rather have...

relationship precognition (know everything that's about to happen)

OR

relationship postcognition (know everything your partner has done)?

YOU MUST CHOOSE!

Authors' Debate

Would you rather...

HAVE PARMESAN CHEESE DANDRUFF

OR

BUBBLE WRAP ACNE?

Authors' Debate

That's a wrap—Justin Heimberg

There are few joys as orgasmically enjoyable as popping bubble wrap. It's irresistibly satisfying. There is something primal about it. It goes back to our evolutionary need to pinch grain or something. Every human has the instinct. Anytime you're bored, you can just pop a bubble zit and get that crackle of satisfaction, either one at a time, or if you have a rather bad breakout, a bunch at once. So, your face will look like a cross between Edward James Olmos and phone packaging. Big deal. Your bubble-pocked face will be smiling ear to ear in joy.

Cheese Please—David Gomberg

Bubble wrap acne has no function. It is a useless deformity. Parmesan cheese dandruff, on the other hand, is wonderfully utilitarian. Parmesan goes well on anything, and a little goes a long way. So if you're out in a restaurant and you get some chicken parmesan, all it takes is a shake of the head, and you're good. Who wants to be addicted to popping their own face? People go through years of therapy for that. Pizza, pasta, vegetables all come alive with a little of the magic from your head and shoulders.

Would you rather...

BE A SUPER VILLAIN CALLED "THE PHARMACIST"

OR

THE GOD OF UPHOLSTERY?

CHAPTER **7** SEVEN

Celebrities and Pop Culture
(To the Extreme, Incidentally)

Our extreme culture has an extreme obsession with extreme celebrity.
Extremely so. How many communal hours of potential productivity
have been sacrificed to worship those who are famous merely for doing
something extreme, be it garish displays of wealth or masochistic acts
on skateboards? It's time to put that pop culture addiction to use and
choose between two famous-folk fates.

Would you rather...

talk like Donald Trump

OR

have his hair?

Would you rather...

have the *Saturday Night Live* guy appear to introduce you whenever you meet new people

OR

have the voice in your head sound like Optimus Prime?

YOU MUST CHOOSE!

Would you rather...

look like Gene Simmons

OR

think like him?

Would you rather...

be a Siamese twin with Nicole Richie

OR

LeBron James?

Would you rather...

have your mom and her friends star on a reality show called "Real Housewives of (Your Home City)"

OR

not?

YOU MUST CHOOSE!

Would you rather...

make out with Tila Tequila

OR

slap her?

Would you rather your mom be...

Marge Simpson **OR** Lois Griffin?

one of the *Desperate Housewives* **OR** *Real Housewives?*

an ornate totem pole **OR** Ann Coulter?

Would you rather your dad be...

Bill Clinton **OR** Richard Gere?

Ru Paul **OR** Ron Paul?

Hulk Hogan **OR** Gandalf?

YOU MUST CHOOSE!

Would you rather spend a long car ride with...

the *Real Housewives of New Jersey* **OR** the *Real Housewives of Orange County?*

Jared of Subway fame **OR** the Hamburglar?

Plato **OR** Tiger Woods?

Would you rather...

have Jessica Simpson's intellect

OR

Jessica Alba's insatiable need (and respective inability) to be funny?

Things to consider: how difficult Alba makes it for men to masturbate to her in her comedies

YOU MUST CHOOSE!

Would you rather be trapped as a character inside...

Gossip Girl **OR** *Grey's Anatomy?*

Lost **OR** *The View?*

The A-Team **OR** *The Office?*

Would you rather...

have to sit through a drunken tirade from Mel Gibson

OR

a serious religious sermon from Tom Cruise?

Would you rather elect as president...

Sarah Palin

OR

Tina Fey?

YOU MUST CHOOSE!

Would you rather...

only be able to leave voicemails in the style and manner of an angry Alec Baldwin

OR

only be able to get your hair cut in the style of an angst-ridden Britney Spears?

Would you rather...

know the truth behind every aspect of Michael Jackson's life

OR

not?

Would you rather...

sit on a transatlantic flight next to Will Ferrell

OR

Oprah?

Things to consider: conversation, mutual armrest competition

YOU MUST CHOOSE!

Would you rather...

have a star on the Walk of Fame

OR

have a deli sandwich named after you?

Would you rather...

have James Taylor living in your closet to help sing your children to sleep

OR

have Pantera in the closet to help wake them up?

YOU MUST CHOOSE!

Would you rather...

have to marry someone at least 40 years your elder like Soon-Yi did with Woody Allen

OR

20 years your younger like Demi Moore did with Ashton Kutcher?
Things to consider: immaturity, gray pubes

Would you rather...

always have the intense facial expression of a runway model

OR

always have the eerie smiling expression of the Burger King mascot?

Would you rather...

have to get everywhere by Big Wheel

OR

by a ball hopper?

YOU MUST CHOOSE!

Would you rather...

have Wolverine hair

OR

wolverine hair?

Would you rather...

be the personal assistant to Donald Trump

OR

Naomi Campbell?

Things to consider: getting fired, getting tired

Would you rather...

be stuck in a bomb shelter with 100 math nerds

OR

with Emeril Lagasse and Joan Rivers?

YOU MUST CHOOSE!

Would you rather...

poop out of your belly-button

OR

through Alex Trebek's?

Would you rather...

roll up into a ball like an armadillo when scared

OR

shake your butt like Shakira?

YOU MUST CHOOSE!

Would you rather...

move like a dancing Gwen Stefani whenever you walk

OR

sway and stomp like Dave Matthews when standing?

Would you rather...

have Popeye's forearms

OR

his cheeks? How about his mental retardation/speech problems or his horrid violent temper and probable alcoholism?

Would you rather...

have permanent Dizzy Gillespie cheeks

OR

speak in jazz scat?

YOU MUST CHOOSE!

Would you rather upon meeting new people...

always cheek-kiss **OR** high five?

hug **OR** low ten?

do that thing where you lock hands and look in and it looks like a vagina **OR** to kiss your biceps and welcome them to the "gun show"?

Would you rather...

be forced to have product placement in your conversations
OR
have to spell out all the words you speak?

Would you rather...

be able to travel via personal Segway
OR
with blades that emerge from your hat, *Inspector Gadget* style?

YOU MUST CHOOSE!

Would you rather...

be bcc'ed on every email to and from Hillary Clinton **OR** Kobe Bryant?

Jennifer Aniston **OR** Ozzy Osbourne?

the Olsen twins **OR** Weird Al Yankovic?

Would you rather...

have to conduct all business meetings in a Spencer's Gifts

OR

in a car parked at Inspiration Point?

Would you rather fight to the death...

a group of sports mascots **OR** cereal mascots?

the last panda on earth **OR** your least favorite relative?

500 possessed protractors **OR** 50 Smurfs?

YOU MUST CHOOSE!

Would you rather...

name your kids something weird and pretentious like celebrities often do

OR

name them "La'Your Name'"?

Things to consider: Which celebrity baby name do you like/hate most?

Would you rather...

have everything you eat taste like Bit-O-Honey

OR

everything you drink taste like Purplesaurus Rex Kool-Aid?

Would you rather...

have gratuitous Nick Cannon cameos in your life

OR

have the sound of studio applause emanate whenever you accomplish something or make a good decision?

YOU MUST CHOOSE!

Would you rather...

be roommates with Jack Tripper

OR

neighbors with Ray Romano?

Would you...

sell space on your body for a tattoo advertisement for $500,000?
Your gravestone? Your child's name?
Things to consider: Nike Heimberg, Abercrombie Fitch Gomberg

Would you rather...

have sex with a soft and tender Toucan Sam

OR

a freaky, furious Cocoa Puffs bird?

YOU MUST CHOOSE!

Would you rather fight to the death...

Fat Albert **OR** Simon and Garfunkel?

a possessed George Foreman grill **OR** an evil version of yourself?

one sober Jean-Claude Van Damme **OR** three drunk Jean-Claude Van Dammes?

Would you rather...

have a massive back tattoo of Queen Latifah

OR

a tattoo of an ampersand on your forehead?

YOU MUST CHOOSE!

Would you rather...

use a razor blade with just one blade

OR

one with 19 blades?

Would you rather...

get caught in a hailstorm of D&D dice

OR

poppers?

YOU MUST CHOOSE!

Would you rather always have to wear...

an eye patch **OR** a nicotine patch?

a snowboard **OR** a Green Lantern outfit?

cataract-protective glasses **OR** kneepads?

Would you rather your graduation speaker be...

Paris Hilton **OR** Gallagher?

Dennis Miller **OR** a happy Asian guy who barely speaks English?

Barack Obama **OR** Optimus Prime?
Things to consider: "Class of 2012, Roll out!"

YOU MUST CHOOSE!

Would you rather...

HAVE SEX WITH CELEBRITIES WITH LAST NAMES THAT BEGIN WITH "L"

OR

LAST NAMES THAT BEGIN WITH "B"?

Authors' Debate

L—Justin Heimberg

Lohan, Liu, Lawless, Landry, Lavigne, Lindvall, Lima, Longoria, Lopez, Borgnine

B2B—David Gomberg

Biel, Bellucci, Bundchen, Braxton, Bullock, Barrymore, Banks, Beckham, Big-ones, Lundgren

EXTRA EXTREMELY EXTREME EXTRAS:

Things to Give Kids on Halloween to Disappoint Them

Miniature alcohol bottles like they have on airplanes

Lamb chops

Autographed photographs of Federal Reserve Chairman Ben Bernanke

A ladleful of gravy

A deed to a fictional ranch

Silks and spices the likes of which they've never seen

Shaving scum

Flotsam and/or Jetsam

Spalding Gray Monologue tapes

YOU MUST CHOOSE!

CHAPTER **8** EIGHT

Extremely Feminine

If you're a dude, turn to the next chapter. *To the extreme!*
Or if in mixed company, pay attention to the answers so you can
understand what women really want.

Would you rather...

never fight with your partner

OR

fight once a week and have great make-up sex?

Would you rather...

have a compulsion that causes you to invariably refer to your breasts as "my jiggle set"

OR

always refer to your vagina as "my love canyon"?

Things to consider: doctor's appointments, writing love letters, getting work at *Penthouse*

Would you rather have a partner with...

a perfect face **OR** a 9-inch penis?

a 2-inch wide, 3-inch long penis **OR** a half-inch wide, 10-inch long penis?

a ribbed-for-your-pleasure penis **OR** a snake tongue?

YOU MUST CHOOSE!

Would you rather...

have sex with John Goodman

OR

assume his weight?

Would you rather...

have sex with Ben Affleck if he gained 50 pounds

OR

Ashton Kutcher if he was speaking the entire time?

Would you rather...

buy seven cucumbers and three boxes of Vagisil at the supermarket right in front of your neighbor

OR

be a nude model for a kindergarten art class?

YOU MUST CHOOSE!

Would you rather...

own a pair of heels that adjusted to flats with the push of a button

OR

a handbag that was able to carry up to 100 pounds without feeling any heavier?

Would you rather...

be smacked in the face with an Andy Roddick serve and then make out with him

OR

get kicked in the stomach by David Beckham and then grope each other feverishly?

Would you rather fart...

in front of your husband/boyfriend **OR** in front of your parents?

in front of your infant child **OR** your pet?

in front of Dame Judi Dench **OR** the ghost of Thomas Jefferson?

YOU MUST CHOOSE!

Would you rather...

have "man hands"

OR

"man feet"?

Would you rather have breasts the consistency of...

softballs **OR** partially-wadded tin foil?

a bag of Frosted Flakes **OR** a sack of wine?

soap bubbles **OR** solid brass?

Would you rather...

have an upside-down vagina **OR** a horizontal vagina?

two vaginas **OR** an anus and vagina that have switched places?

a vagina that can act as a blowdryer **OR** a vacuum?

YOU MUST CHOOSE!

Would you rather...

get in a catfight with Miley Cyrus

OR

Ne-Ne from *Real Housewives: Atlanta?*

Would you rather...

find out your coveted collection of Jimmy Choo handbags were all cheap knock-offs

OR

your real designer bags were made by slave-like child labor?

Would you rather...

be caricatured by Kristen Wiig on *Saturday Night Live*

OR

have *Us Weekly* regularly photograph you and make fun of your wardrobe in its *Fashion Police* section?

YOU MUST CHOOSE!

Would you rather...

have your boobs drop six inches overnight

OR

your butt drop six inches overnight?

Would you rather...

get a haircut in the style of Dorothy Hamill

OR

Dorothy from *The Wizard of Oz*?

Would you rather...

on your wedding day, accidentally say an old boyfriend's name during your vows

OR

after walking down the aisle to make your entrance, realize you have skidmarks on your wedding dress?

YOU MUST CHOOSE!

Would you rather...

fellate a guy with a 14-inch penis while you're suffering from a sore throat

OR

receive anal sex from a guy with a 2-inch diameter penis?

Things to consider: This question excerpted from Chaucer's *Canterbury Tales*

Would you rather...

have sex with Mel Gibson **OR** Kevin Federline?

John Mayer **OR** Ryan Reynolds?

Josh Groban **OR** Kanye West?

the character of Dr. House **OR** the character of Chuck from *Gossip Girl*?

a sea lion **OR** Dick Cheney?

YOU MUST CHOOSE!

Would you rather...

have the ability to instantly make your breasts the size of your choice

OR

have a butt capable of altering size and shape to fit into any pair of pants (but only while you are wearing the pants)?
Things to consider: disrobing for sex, jogging

Would you rather...

your partner have a one-inch penis

OR

the most perfect penis; however it's jutting out of his lower back? His neck? The bottom of his left foot?

Would you rather...

tattoo Bret Michaels's name on your forehead

OR

have unprotected sex with him and just hope for the best?

YOU MUST CHOOSE!

Would you rather...

at bars, constantly be hit on by every guy no matter how lame he is

OR

always have to make the first move?

Date, Marry, or Screw?

Tom Cruise, Johnny Depp, Barack Obama

Anderson Cooper, the Pick-Up Artist, Seth Rogen

Michael Kors, Tom Colicchio, The Incredible Hulk

YOU MUST CHOOSE!

Would you...

never send another text message to have sex with George Clooney?

Would you...

eat your next 50 meals at McDonald's to grope Justin Timberlake?

Would you...

have your breasts surgically altered so that one was a B-cup and the other was a DDD-cup to have Josh Hartnett as a sex slave?

YOU MUST CHOOSE!

Would you rather suffer the fate of...

Joan of Arc

OR

Katie Holmes?

Would you rather...

have self-renewing shoes

OR

have self-applying make-up?

Would you rather your boyfriend be...

Cojo **OR** Steve-O?

Dwight Yoakam **OR** Dwight Schrute?

Michael Phelps **OR** Criss Angel?

YOU MUST CHOOSE!

Would you rather...

be the fourth Kardashian sister

OR

the third Hilton sister?

Would you rather...

hook up with everyone Nicole Kidman has ever hooked up with

OR

everyone Jennifer Aniston has ever hooked up with?

Would you rather...

have Kim Kardashian's ass but uncontrollably fart all the time

OR

Salma Hayek's breasts but uncontrollably lactate all the time?

Would you rather...

receive a new piece of Tiffany's jewelry every month

OR

receive oral sex from Colin Farrell on your command?

YOU MUST CHOOSE!

Would you rather live in a world...

where women earned on average 25% more than men

OR

where men experienced menstrual cycles, symptoms and cramps?

Would you rather live in a world...

where men took their wives' last names upon marriage

OR

where couples chose a new last name together?

Things to consider: Maury Chung, Matthew Parker, Mr. and Mrs. Lightning

Would you rather have a 3-way with...

Ben and Casey Affleck **OR** Mark and Donnie Wahlberg?

Fred and Ben Savage **OR** Jerry and Charlie O'Connell?

Noel and Liam Gallagher **OR** the AFLAC Duck and the Kool-Aid Man?

YOU MUST CHOOSE!

Would you rather permanently ban the word...

"ho" **OR** "dyke"?

"panties" **OR** "bromance"?

the C-word **OR** the N-word?

"windy" **OR** "challenge"?

If it meant having a flawless body, would you give up...

eating utensils?

vowels?

carbon-based sexual partners?

YOU MUST CHOOSE!

Would you rather...

if forced to do so on national TV, with your current abilities, have the chance to nationally disprove the "women are bad drivers" stereotype

OR

the "bad at math" stereotype?

Would you rather...

be able to manicure nails by sucking on fingers

OR

pedicure nails by sucking on toes?
Things to consider: doing your own nails, working at a salon

Would you rather...

have access to the world's only honest mechanic

OR

the world's hottest gynecologist?

YOU MUST CHOOSE!

Would you rather...

have an index finger that blended perfect margaritas and other mixed drinks

OR

have card-shuffling cleavage?

Would you rather...

have your significant other love to sleep, holding, cuddling, and touching you

OR

never have blanket tugging issues?

Would you rather...

receive an all-expense paid trip to Paris but have your travel partner be a two year-old child you have to look after

OR

spend a luxury private-island escape in Fiji with Flava Flav?

YOU MUST CHOOSE!

Would you rather...

be able to cause couples to break up by focusing your negative energy on them

OR

be capable of causing couples to form?

Would you rather...

have towelettes that can wipe away wrinkles

OR

ones that can wipe away memories of bad relationships?

Would you rather...

the National Debt Clock in Times Square instead display your weight at all times

OR

the JumboTron at Madison Square Garden play a video of your daily grooming and waxing?

YOU MUST CHOOSE!

Would you rather...

only be able to have sex with John Goodman until you orgasm in the act

OR

only be allowed to eat dice until you pooped a 7?

Would you rather...

be the CEO of a Fortune 500 company

OR

the spouse of one?
Things to consider: Be honest

Would you rather...

work off of a computer from 1978

OR

have to dress in the fashion of 1978?
Things to consider: green text, green bellbottoms

YOU MUST CHOOSE!

Would you rather...

work under 1985 office dress codes

OR

1955 office politics?

Things to consider: feathered hair, expectant ass-slapping, "Thanks, babe!"

Without anyone finding out, would you sleep with your boss for...

a promotion?

a fully paid, 4-day work week?

a fully paid, 3-day work week?

a gorgeous private work bathroom?

a job title of "Royal Highness"?

Would you rather...

increase your annual salary by $1,000

OR

permanently reduce someone else's (your choice) by $10,000?

YOU MUST CHOOSE!

Would you rather...

have an office kitty

OR

an office hottie?

Things to consider: tongue baths, visible scratches

Would you rather...

realize after your first day at work that you were showing serious thong "whale tale"

OR

give a thoughtful presentation only to then realize you had a serious case of nipple-itis during the whole thing?

Things to consider: Both happened to Madeline Albright

Would you rather...

find out all your emails were being monitored and read by your boss

OR

that all your moments at your desk were being filmed by a security camera?

YOU MUST CHOOSE!

Would you rather...

have sex with this guy

OR this guy?

YOU MUST CHOOSE!

EXTRA EXTREMELY EXTREME EXTRAS:

5 Events if There Were an Autumn Olympics

Speed-raking

Synchronized Pumpkin Carving

Leaf Pile Floor Exercise

Cider-Mulling for Accuracy

Biathlon: Distance Run through Forest; Foliage Appreciation

YOU MUST CHOOSE!

9

Extremely Masculine

Okay, so here's where all the extra extreme extraneous questions about balls and porn and sports fall into. What may seem a bit extreme to the fairer sex is just everyday conversation for guys. If you're a lady, you may want to move on, or you may find what guys have to say in this chapter extremely interesting… and perhaps interestingly extreme? No? Anyone? That was a nice turn of phrase. Screw you…
to the extreme!

Would you rather...

get five hours of conversation with Barack Obama

OR

five minutes of wild sex with Jessica Alba?

Would you rather...

your only porn be toilet paper commercials

OR

1983 high school yearbooks?

Would you rather...

date someone on a perpetual period

OR

with perpetual PMS?

YOU MUST CHOOSE!

Would you rather...

have Internet chat sex only to find out it was your aunt (she discovers it was you too)

OR

receive a great glory hole BJ only to then realize it was former NBA great Ralph Sampson on the other side of the wall?

Would you rather...

have the old Boston Garden parquet floor in your living room

OR

a backyard that is a replica of Hole 7 at Augusta National Golf Club?

Would you rather...

have testicles that literally drag on the floor when you're naked

OR

testicles that zig and zag around wildly like nuclear particles?

Things to consider: stuffing your sock, freeballing

YOU MUST CHOOSE!

Would you rather have sex with...

Eva Mendes **OR** Alicia Keys?

Mary Louise Parker **OR** Kendra Wilkinson, but you have to talk with her for two hours before?

Heidi Klum **OR** Heidi Montag?

Maria Sharapova with full grunting **OR** Lauren Conrad on mute?

Eva Longoria **OR** Vanessa Hudgens?

YOU MUST CHOOSE!

Would you rather...

have a penis that could be detached and attached (with sensitivity) to any part of your body

OR

have a penis that could be played like a flute?

Would you rather...

see you parents' room's stains exposed with a blacklight

OR

have your parents expose your room?

Things to consider: You and your parents would both be present during the reveal.

Would you rather...

when passing by people, be compelled to guard them as if playing basketball

OR

have an insatiable compulsion to knock things out of children's hands?

YOU MUST CHOOSE!

Would you rather...

have sex with a mermaid

OR

with a reverse mermaid (upper half = big fish, lower half = woman)?

Would you rather...

have softball-sized testicles

OR

softball-sized breasts?

Would you rather...

turn into Paul Revere during foreplay

OR

turn into Jerry Lewis upon orgasm?

Would you rather...

have self-lubricating genitals

OR

be able to dunk two-handed?

YOU MUST CHOOSE!

Would you rather...

have a bowling alley in your house

OR

have a device resembling a bowling alley ball-returner that refills empty beer mugs?

Would you rather...

see an action movie set in a Bed, Bath and Beyond

OR

at a Panera's Breads and Bakery?

Would you rather...

have penises for fingers

OR

a finger for your penis?

YOU MUST CHOOSE!

Would you rather...

have to drive three times the speed limit

OR

1/3 the speed limit?

Would you rather...

die by drowning yourself in your toilet

OR

by consuming roll after roll of Charmin?

Would you rather have sex with...

Carrie Underwood **OR** Kristen Bell?

Beyoncé **OR** Rihanna?

Danica Patrick **OR** Fergie?

your hottest high school teacher **OR** Eliza Dushku?

YOU MUST CHOOSE!

Would you rather...

have a girlfriend with speedbag breasts you could practice your boxing on

OR

with a heavy bag back?

Would you rather...

be cross-eyed

OR

cross-balled?

Would you rather...

regularly experience nocturnal emission

OR

a nocturnal admission (where once a night you admit something embarrassing in your sleep)?

YOU MUST CHOOSE!

Would you rather...

have sex with Jenna Jameson

OR

Jenna Haze

OR

Jenna Fischer?

Would you rather...

be the sixth man off the bench for an NBA team but get no money

OR

receive an NBA salary but have to keep your current job?

Would you rather fight...

a rhino with a machine gun

OR

a rabid dog without any weapons?

YOU MUST CHOOSE!

Would you rather...

have to wear a yarmulke on your head

OR

a mini yarmulke on your penis head?

Would you rather...

Charles Barkley **OR** a barber shop quartet?

a polar bear **OR** 3 Yao Ming clones?

11 possessed trombones **OR** 10,000 fire flies?

Would you rather...

have a music playlist sent to you that is scientifically proven to increase exercise performance

OR

a playlist that is scientifically proven to help you get laid?

YOU MUST CHOOSE!

Would you rather...

only be able to pee on cop cars

OR

only be able to crap by flagpoles?

Would you rather date a girl with...

junk in the trunk **OR** fats in the lats?

a rose in the nose **OR** wheat in the feet?

(Pirates) maps on the traps **OR** pegs for the legs?

Would you rather...

trade lives with Conan O'Brien

OR

Dwayne Wade?

YOU MUST CHOOSE!

Would you rather...

have Jay Leno's money but also his chin

OR

have Letterman's money but also his outlook on life?

Would you rather...

have a panther that obeys your every command and does your bidding **OR** 500 bees that do the same?

a pack of dolphins **OR** a trio of former NBA seven footers?

a king cobra **OR** a Muppet?

Would you rather...

have sex with Dakota Fanning in seven years

OR

Jennifer Love Hewitt twelve years ago?

YOU MUST CHOOSE!

Pick your penis!
Would you rather have...

a candy cane shaped penis **OR** a corkscrew shaped penis?

a hammerhead penis **OR** a Phillips screwdriver head to your penis?

a Pez-dispensing penis **OR** a penis that shoots out a little flag that says "bang" upon orgasm?

Would you rather live in a world where...

whoever denied it, supplied it

OR

whoever smelt it, dealt it?

YOU MUST CHOOSE!

Would you rather...

fight Zach Braff

OR

Zac Efron?

Would you rather be stuck on a deserted island with...

Aristotle **OR** Megan Fox?

Dave Chappelle **OR** Sacha Baron Cohen?

Simon Cowell **OR** an electronic Simon game?
Things to consider: going mad

Tom Colicchio **OR** Lindsay Lohan?

Moses **OR** Moses Malone?
Things to consider: playing one on one

YOU MUST CHOOSE!

Would you rather change your name to...

Porp **OR** Aragorn?

Narkath the Bloated **OR** Zorzootz 9?

the smell of toffee **OR** the sound of change jingling?

Would you rather...

have your cell phone set on racist joke

OR

stench of taint?

Would you rather...

have a 14 second metabolism from eating to excretion

OR

every five minutes, have the place where you're standing explode, so you got to get the hell out of there like an action hero?

Things to consider: toilet chairs, nomadic life

YOU MUST CHOOSE!

Would you rather...

only be sexually excited by the sounds of foghorns

OR

have genitalia set to explode the day you turn 70?

Would you rather...

be a man with 38DDs

OR

be a man with a one-inch penis?

YOU MUST CHOOSE!

Would you rather...

summarily execute all DJs

OR

all reality stars?

Would you rather...

have your self-esteem hinge on the L.A. Clippers road record

OR

have your happiness dependent on the bounty of an Alaskan crabbing ship?

Would you rather...

be able to park in handicap places

OR

be able to make fun of the retarded with no guilt or repercussions?

YOU MUST CHOOSE!

Would you rather...

have a Real Doll of Megan Fox

OR

a voodoo doll of your most hated male celebrity?

Would you rather...

have your profanity magically dubbed with less offensive words

OR

have everything you hear delayed like you are off reporting via satellite (you have to hold your ear to hear and nod like they do as well)?

Which of the following email addresses would you rather use...

scrotationdevice@gmail.com **OR** johnnydoodoo@aol.com?

ballslikeavocados@tmail.com **OR** saggysac@gmail.com?

fartonyourface@yahoo.com **OR** racismisok@hotmail.com?

YOU MUST CHOOSE!

Would you rather...

always deliver the perfect toast, balanced with poignancy

OR

be able to shoot pencils with your belly fat with the force and accuracy of a bow and arrow?

Would you rather...

always have a parking spot open up when you need it

OR

always be able to reach into your pocket and have exact change?

Would you rather...

be wasted at your child's birthday party

OR

your parents' anniversary dinner?

Would you...

spend ten minutes in the octagon with *Ultimate Fighting* giant Brock Lesnar for ten minutes in bed with Adriana Lima?

YOU MUST CHOOSE!

International House of Dilemmas
Would you rather...

eat only British food **OR** have British teeth?

have to always sit Indian style **OR** always have French B.O.?

live in a society that dressed in togas **OR** in feathered headdresses?

Would you rather...

be incredibly charming but always have a dump in your pants

OR

be extremely witty but feel compelled to intermittently spread peanut butter all over your arm?

Would you rather...

marry the Octomom

OR

be raised by her?

YOU MUST CHOOSE!

Would you rather...

write all work-related emails in the voice of an eighth grade girl full of IM abbreviations, smileys, and "like"s

OR

in the voice of a weirdly articulate revolutionary soldier's letter as in "Today at the meeting, I met a man to whose countenance men were beholden." ?

Would you rather...

have a comb-over from your chest hair

OR

ear hair? Eyelashes?

Would you rather...

have to masturbate with a mitten

OR

with your off-hand?

YOU MUST CHOOSE!

Would you rather...

when older, smoke a pipe
OR
cigars?

Gun to your head, if you had to have sex with a guy, who would you choose?

YOU MUST CHOOSE!

Extreme Fantasies

"Extreme fantasy" is a redundancy. You don't tend to have fantasies of pleasant, though unexceptional sex, and you don't dream about being the second string quarterback signaling in plays from the sidelines. Then again, to each his own. The following fantasies run the gamut from mild to wild. Use extreme discretion in choosing.

Would you rather always be...

16 **OR** 35?

12 **OR** 50?

2 **OR** 72?

Would you rather have sex with...

a virgin **OR** a porn star?

Jessicas Biel, Alba, and Simpson **OR** Jennifers Lopez, Garner, and Love Hewitt?

Wilma Flintstone **OR** Betty Rubble?

YOU MUST CHOOSE!

Would you rather have sex with...

George Clooney ten years ago **OR** Johnny Depp ten years from now?

a bad boy **OR** a choir boy?

Big Bird **OR** Megatron?

Would you rather...

watch a show called "The Biggest Luger"

OR

"Alzheimer's Patients Say the Darnedest Things"?

Would you rather spend a day with...

Terry Bradshaw **OR** Fred Armisen?

Al Franken **OR** Al Pacino?

Gary Gnu **OR** Will. I. Am?

YOU MUST CHOOSE!

Would you rather...

have an hour of conversation with Jesus

OR

an hour of wild sex with the celebrity of your choice?

Would you rather split a bottle of whiskey with...

Tommy Lee **OR** Stephen Hawking?

Howie Mandel **OR** Bilbo Baggins?

Malcolm X **OR** the Incredible Hulk?

Would you rather your partner...

compliment you

OR

complement you?

YOU MUST CHOOSE!

Would you rather...

smoke pot with Colin Powell

OR

Steven Spielberg?

Would you rather live in a world...

where humans engage in a jump ball to determine all disagreements

OR

where they play Rock Paper Scissors?

Would you rather...

be able to tap the phone of a celebrity of your choice

OR

an acquaintance of your choice?

YOU MUST CHOOSE!

Would you rather interview...

Thomas Edison **OR** Mother Teresa?

George Washington **OR** George Clooney?

a wasted Pat O'Brien **OR** a wasted Joe Namath?

Would you rather...

have a bowl of oatmeal with Charles Barkley

OR

dam a creek with Matt Lauer?

Would you rather...

catch crickets with Ben Kingsley

OR

construct a sofa fort with Michael Douglas?

YOU MUST CHOOSE!

Would you rather...

take a road trip with Socrates, Patrick Ewing, and Steve Carell

OR

your mom, Thomas Paine, and John Belushi?

Would you rather...

have Bobby Flay as your personal chef

OR

your choice of Angelina Jolie or Brad Pitt as your personal sex slave?

YOU MUST CHOOSE!

Would you rather...

LIVE IN A WORLD COMPOSED ENTIRELY OF NERF

OR

TOOTSIE ROLL?

Would you rather...

get to be a guest judge on *American Idol*

OR

get to force one of your friends to go on it?

Would you rather...

have a comic book superhero based on you

OR

a reality show based on your life?

Things to consider: What would your powers be?

Would you rather...

have sex with Josh Duhamel and get genital warts

OR

have sex with Bryant Gumble and get a Louis Vuitton bag?

YOU MUST CHOOSE!

Would you rather...

have sex with Marisa Miller and get scurvy

OR

have sex with Joy Behar and get season tickets to your favorite football team?

Would you rather have sex with...

a 10 **OR** a 7 and a 3 at the same time?

ten 1's **OR** five 2's?

a 3, a 9, and a 1 **OR** a 4 and an 8?
Things to consider: Which bowling spare would you rather face?

Would you rather...

have a wise black caddy always hanging around to give you homespun advice

OR

have an unlimited supply of taffy?

YOU MUST CHOOSE!

Would you rather...

LIVE IN THE STAR TREK UNIVERSE

OR

THE WORLD OF DR. SEUSS?

Would you rather...

go to Vegas with Einstein

OR

Shakespeare?
Things to consider: card-counting, picking up chicks

Would you rather have it be...

Christmas every day **OR** Thanksgiving?

your wedding day **OR** a friend's wedding day?

a Bar-mitzvah **OR** Arbor Day?

Would you rather...

go to outer space

OR

have a threesome with two hot twins?

YOU MUST CHOOSE!

Would you rather...

have a staring contest with the Pope

OR

play ping pong against Kim Jong-il?

Would you rather...

have a street named after you

OR

have a martial art developed based on your physical style?
Things to consider: What would it be called, look like?

Would you rather...

be able to change a physical feature of yourself

OR

of your partner?

YOU MUST CHOOSE!

Would you rather have a bedroom designed by...

the people that make James Bond contraptions **OR** MC Escher?

Dr. Seuss **OR** Frank Lloyd Wright?

Would you rather...

have Ken Burns make a 14 part miniseries about your life full of low-key interviews and pan-dissolves

OR

have Michelangelo make a sculpture of you?

YOU MUST CHOOSE!

Would you rather have a different one-of-a-kind outfit designed for you every day by...

Christian Siriano **OR** Zac Posen?

Ralph Lauren **OR** Givenchy?

Dolce & Gabanna **OR** Stella McCartney?

Would you rather...

have lived the life of James Madison **OR** Wilt Chamberlain?

Paul McCartney **OR** Derek Jeter?

your mom **OR** your dad?

YOU MUST CHOOSE!

CHAPTER ELEVEN

WHAT WOULD YOU BE?
How to Use This Chapter

Game 1: *I Am Thinking of Someone We All Know.*
This is a way to use this chapter as a group game. One player thinks of someone who everybody in the group knows: a friend, a coworker, an enemy, a teacher, etc. This is the "name on the table." Other players take turns reading a randomly selected page of questions from this chapter. The player who is thinking of someone answers each question as if he were that person. After every page, have a player guess who you are thinking of.
Optional: If you want, you can all write down a bunch of people you know on scraps of paper, turn them over, and have the answerer pull a name from the pile.

Game 2: *Conversation.*

Pretty simple. Read a question and answer it as yourself. If there is a group of you, everybody should answer the question. Suggest your own answers for what you think others are and discuss why. See who agrees and who disagrees. Debate. Deliberate. Arm-wrestle. Think about other people you know (your friends, family, bosses, etc.) and what they would be. When the conversation fades into silence and awkward stares—you guessed it—it's time to move on to the next question.

Game 3: *Celebrity.*

Go back a page. Reread the directions for Game 1, but substitute "celebrity" for "someone who everybody in the group knows."

Game 4: *Ninja Strike.*

Find a horde of bandits marauding caravans. Train in the martial arts, specializing in book warfare. Fashion this book into a throwing star or other deadly piece of weaponry. Defeat marauders.

If you were a **color,** what would you be?

If you were a **dog**, what breed would you be? What would your bark sound like?

If you were a *Simpsons character*, who would you be?

If you were a **type of car**, what make and model would you be? What condition are you in? How many miles do you have on you?

YOU MUST CHOOSE!

If you were a punctuation mark, what would you be?
A few to choose from: ? ! ; * , / ( ) $ & . and don't forget the versatile #, the smug ^ , or the wily ~

If you were a beat, what would you be? (Drum it or beatbox it.)

If you were a type of cheese, what would you be?

If you were a member of the A-Team, which character would you be?
Things to consider: Are you crazy? Are you slick and good-looking? Do you enjoy the culmination of a plan? Are you a large black man with a Mohawk who wears a preposterous amount of jewelry and has an aversion to air travel?

YOU MUST CHOOSE!

If you were a weather forecast, what would you be? Give the forecast as if a weatherman: For example, "Mostly sunny with a chance of afternoon thunderstorms. Some storms might be severe, becoming cooler at night…"

If you were a state, which would you be?

Things to consider: Are you dry? Hot? Do you have a panhandle?

If you were a Beatle, which one would you be?

If you were a tattoo, what would you be and on what part of the body?

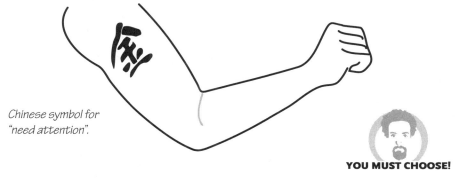

Chinese symbol for "need attention".

YOU MUST CHOOSE!

Physical Phun!

If you were a facial expression, what would you be? (Make it.)

If you were a walk (a strut, a trot, an affected limp for sympathy, *etc.*), what would you be? (Walk it.)

If you were a sexual position, what would you be? (Demonstrate it with five thrusts. Use another person if need be.)

Question of character

If you had to partake in sexual role-playing, what fantasy would appeal to you most: a) "Teacher Keeps Bookish Student after Class"; b) "Football Player Meets Cheerleader in Locker Room"; or c) "Post-Roast Beef Sandwich Consumption Run-in with Anonymous Thin Moroccan in Arby's Bathroom Stall"?

YOU MUST CHOOSE!

If you were a **font**, which would you be?

Tiki Surf

Serpentine

META - BOLD CAPS

Balzano

RUBBER STAMP

boycott   Jokerman

Cat Krap

Tekton Pro Bold

σψμβολ

Whimsy ICG

Funky Western

Interstate Hairline

Did you know?

The font that gets laid the most is *French Script*, while **Goudy Stout** is gay. Bauhaus and Lucida Sans Unicode are both virgins.

YOU MUST CHOOSE!

If you were a finger, which would you be (Pinky, Ring, Middle, Index, Thumb)?

If you were a movie genre, what would you be? What would your Motion Picture Association movie rating be? (G, PG, R, etc.)

If you were a city, which would you be?
Things to consider: Are you fast-paced? Laid-back? Do you have a giant arch protruding from you?

If you were a painting, what would you be? If you can't think of any, choose between *The Starry Night* by Vincent Van Gogh, a calm landscape scene of an ocean with a lighthouse, a wild and abstract Jackson Pollock splatter-painting, or *Dogs Playing Poker*.

YOU MUST CHOOSE!

For the following questions, use your cell phones or PDAs to answer.

If you were a **cell phone ring**, what would you be? Go through your phone's rings until you get the best one.

If you were a **type of cell phone** or **PDA** (iPhone, Blackberry, etc.), what would you be? What if you were a PDA as in public display of affection? (Demonstrate it.)

If you were a **text message using only 5 letters**, what would you be? (Text it.)

Question of character

Who would be your ideal phone sex partner?
Some ideas: Angelina Jolie, Russell Crowe, Jenna Jameson, Lou Dobbs, Marcel Marceau, the *Inside the NFL* guy, Yourself.

YOU MUST CHOOSE!

Are you...

a **Mac** or **PC?**

a **Dog** or **Cat?**

Salt or **Pepper?**

Abbott or **Costello?**

Sugar or **Spice?**

Day or **Night?**

a **Beach** or **Mountain?**

Doo-doo or **Pee-pee?**

YOU MUST CHOOSE!

If you were a gem or precious stone, what would you be?

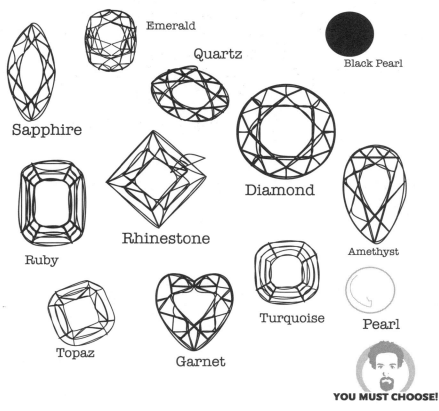

Sapphire

Emerald

Quartz

Black Pearl

Diamond

Ruby

Rhinestone

Amethyst

Topaz

Garnet

Turquoise

Pearl

YOU MUST CHOOSE!

You Are What You Eat!

If you were a bar drink or cocktail, what would you be?
Things to consider: Are you strong? Watered down? Fruity?

If you were a condiment, what would you be?

If you were a dessert, what would you be? What would the nutrition label say?

If you were a cereal, which would you be? How about if you were a cereal mascot?
Things to consider: Why are all cereal mascots either addicts or pushers?

YOU MUST CHOOSE!

If you were a **cartoon character**, who would you be?

If you were a **deodorant scent**, what would you be?
Things to consider: alpine frost, cool breeze, clean blast, tundratastic, salmon

If you were an **exclamation** or **sound made during sex**, what would you be? (Say it like you mean it!)

If you were an **onomatopoeia** (a sound-word like SMACK, THUD, SPLAT, or SQUISH), what would you be?
Things to consider: We hope your answer to this question was not the same as the answer to the previous question.

YOU MUST CHOOSE!

QUIZ 1

Who is this actor?

If he were an animal, he'd be a fox.

If he were an article of clothing, he'd be a tailored suit.

If he were a drink, he'd be a martini.

If he were a movie character, he'd be James Bond.

Answer: George Clooney

If you were any **character from a movie** or **TV show**, who would you be?

If you were a **part of the body**, what would you be?

If you were a **shape**, what would you be? (Draw it.)

If you were any **famous John**, which John would you be?
Things to consider: Do you have a macho Western air about you? Does sunshine on your shoulders make you happy? Do you have large genitals?
Do you have mutilated genitals?

If you were a **famous Jen** or **Jennifer**, who would you be?

YOU MUST CHOOSE!

If you were a **speed limit**, what would you be?

If you were a **type of terrain** (mountains, desert, foothills, etc.), what would you be?

If you were a **piece of furniture**, what would you be?
Things to consider: Are you leather? Worn down? Modern? Classic?

If you were a **candy bar**, what would you be?

Did you know?

The Charleston Chew was invented by the Nazis as a battle snack.*

*Not true.

If you were a **musical instrument**, what would you be?

If you were a **musical note** or **chord**, what would you sound like? (Hum the note or play it if an instrument is near.)

Express who you are in a **drum solo**.

Express who you are by 20 seconds of **air guitar**.

YOU MUST CHOOSE!

If you were a **zoo animal**, what would you be?

If you were a **circus act**, what would you be?

If you were **something in Australia**, what would you be?

If you were a **Greek god**, who would you be?

Question of character

What would you want to be God of if you could be God of something? Fashion? Flatulence? Bad Hair Days? First Dates? Ennui?

YOU MUST CHOOSE!

Gone Hollywood

If you were a movie, what movie would you be?
Some ideas: *When Harry Met Sally, Friday the 13th, Rocky, Pulp Fiction, Big Breast Bangers 8, Big Breast Bangers 9.*

If you were an actor/actress, who would you be?

If you were a Hollywood super couple, who would you be?
Things to consider: TomKat, Brangelina, Bennifer, Fabioprah.

Question of character

If your life were to get an Oscar nomination, what would it be for? Best actor? Best supporting actor? Best writing? Best score? Special effects?

YOU MUST CHOOSE!

If you were a hairstyle, what would you be? Some (but not all) to choose from:

Crew cut
Says: **All business.**

Spiked Mohawk
Says: **"F off."**

Mullet
Says: **Business in the front. Party in the back.**

The Visor
Says: **Party in the front. Business in the back.**

The Afro
Says: **Party everywhere.**

254

Pony tail.

Says: (for women) – **I'm playful and energetic.** (for men) – **I'm sensitive and trying to get laid.**

The Anchorman

Says: **That shouldn't be a problem.**

Middle part
Says: **Precision, symmetry. 1983.**

Jheri Curls
Says: **It all.**

YOU MUST CHOOSE!

If you were a **month**, what would you be?

If you were a **playing card**, what would you be?

If you were a **country**, what would you be?

If you were a **sound**, what would you be?
Things to consider: a foghorn, a last gasp, glass breaking, wind chimes, gong

YOU MUST CHOOSE!

Origa-ME

Tear this page out and make an **origami** (folded paper sculpture) that represents you.

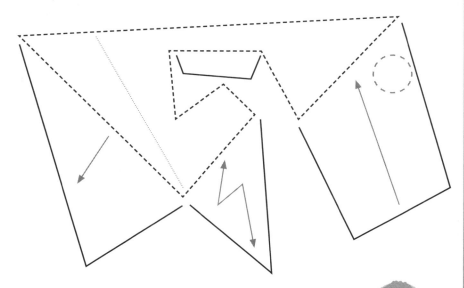

YOU MUST CHOOSE!

Animal Instincts

If you were a creature of the sea, what would you be?

If you were a mammal, what would you be?

If you were an insect, what would you be?

If you were a bird, what would you be?

If you could create an animal that was you, what would it be?

Head of a _____? Body of a _____?

Hands/claws of a _____ ? Mind of a _____?

Courage of a _____?

YOU MUST CHOOSE!

Are you…

a **fork**, **knife**, or **spoon**?

rock, **paper**, or **scissors**?

a **red**, **yellow**, or **green** light?

a **yes**, **no**, or **maybe**?

Larry, **Curly**, or **Moe**?

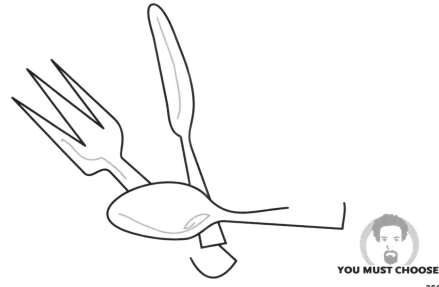

YOU MUST CHOOSE!

If you were a song, what song would you be?
Which rendition? (Sing it.)

If you were a spice, what would you be?

If you were a Spice Girl, which would you be?

If you were a famous historical figure, who would you be?

Did you know?

Confederacy President Jefferson Davis invented the high five.*

*Not true.

YOU MUST CHOOSE!

If you were a **hand tool**, what would you be?

If you were a **flower** or **plant**, what would you be?

If you were a **character in the Bible**, which would you be?

If you were a **video game character**, what character would you be?

Question of character

What if you were a **character in a video game based on the Bible?** How would the game go?
You get points for all the lepers you heal?
All the suffering you can bear? All the outdated passages you interpret literally?

YOU MUST CHOOSE!

261

You Are What You Write

If you were handwriting, what would you be? Write a sentence in the handwriting that captures your essence.

If you were a work of abstract art, what would you be? (Draw it.)

If you were an Instant Message acronym (LOL, BRB, TTYL, etc.), what would you be?

IM acronyms for super villains: MLOL (Maniacal laugh out loud); IWDY (I will destroy you); (BRBBYW) (Be right back, but you won't); ISSATEIAFIRFIWAANWIMOIE (I shall sweep away the Earth in a fiery inferno, recreating from its windblown ashes a new world in my own image everlasting)

YOU MUST CHOOSE!

If you were a **planet**, which one would you be?

Things to consider: the beauty and mystique of Saturn, Jupiter the gas giant, the tempestuous and hot Venus, Uranus.

If you were a **metal**, what would you be?

Things to consider: Are you strong? Lustrous? Precious?

If you were a **curse word**, what would you be? How would you be said? (Demonstrate.)

If you were a **monster**, what would you be?

Things to consider: vampire, zombie, yeti, black pudding, pubic elves, (See "About the Author" for the monster called Gomberg).

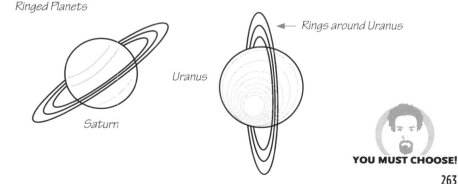

Ringed Planets

Rings around Uranus

Uranus

Saturn

YOU MUST CHOOSE!

QUIZ 2

Who is this celebrity?

If he were a **food**, he'd be cheese.

If he were a **color**, he'd be gold.

If he were a **playing card**, he'd be the Ace of Spades.

If he were a **character from a movie**, he'd be Gordon Gekko.

Answer: Donald Trump

If you were a **Smurf**, who would you be?

If you were **one of the seven dwarves**, which would you be?

If you were **one of the symptoms Nyquil is meant to help with**, which would you be?

If you were a **kickball pitch** ("slow and smooth", "fast and bouncy", etc.), what would you be?

Ambivalent Smurf

YOU MUST CHOOSE!

If you were a **time of the day**, what would you be?

If you were any **character from a book**, who would you be?
Things to consider: Holden Caulfield, Frodo Baggins, Scout, Encyclopedia Brown, Hamlet, Flat Stanley

If you were a **type of building** (hut, skyscraper, wigwam, office park), what would you be?

If you were a **comic strip character**, who would you be?
Things to consider: Dilbert, Garfield, Prince Valiant, Calvin, a Far Side cow, the Would You Rather...? guy (see the book Would You Rather...? Illustrated).

Question of character

If you had a **vanity plate** on your car, what would you have? (Examples: IMCOOL, WADEVA, 2MUCH, ILUVSOD, etc.)

YOU MUST CHOOSE!

Which one of you...

Which one of you or your friends is **Q*bert?**

Which one of you or your friends is a **desert?**

Which one of you or your friends is a **ruby?**

Which one of you or your friends is **The Fonz?**

Which one of you or your friends is **Swing dance?**

If you were a **book genre**, what would you be?

If you were a **morning beverage**, what would you be?

If you were **one of the founding fathers**,
who would you be?
Things to consider: the quiet but brilliant James Madison; the inflexible but eloquent
Jefferson, the bold and commanding Washington, the bloated and problem-flatulent
Templeton.

Did you know?

*The reason John Hancock signed his name larger than
normal on the Declaration of Independence is because
he had hands twice the size of a normal human being.**

*Not true. The real reason he signed so big was because
he was an asshole.

YOU MUST CHOOSE!

Life's a Gamble

If you were a **casino game**, what would you be?

How about if you were a **blackjack hand**?

A **poker hand**?

A **roll of the dice in craps**?

And finally, **finish this slot machine spin**:
Cherry… Cherry… and…

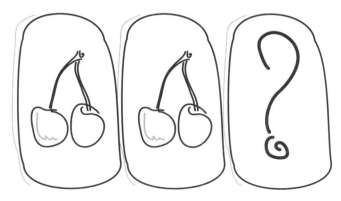

YOU MUST CHOOSE!

Question of character

What's in a Name?

Choose a **name** that best expresses your essence:

If you had a **rapper name**, what would it be?

If you had a **porn star name**, what would it be?

If you had a **pirate name**, what would it be?

If you had a *Dungeons & Dragons* name, what would it be?

If you had a **Mafia name**, what would it be?

YOU MUST CHOOSE!

If you were a **type of vehicle**, what would you be?

If you were a **street in New York City**, what would you be? Describe it in detail.

Things to consider: Wall Street, Park Avenue, a street in the West Village, a Harlem alley.

If you were a **famous landmark**, what would you be?

If you were a **smell**, what would you be?

Things to consider: roses, suntan oil, mulch, tar, new sheets, ass, BBQ, all of the above.

YOU MUST CHOOSE!

12

Extreme Beauty, Body, Appearance and Fashion

Gone are the days where dying your hair blue made you extreme. That's downright conformist these days. To be avant-garde now means piercing your nose with a chain connected to a live mallard or getting a full body tattoo of an elk raping a walrus. With these new standards of extreme in mind, we present to you some choices in forward-thinking fashion and bodywork.

Would you rather...

get a face lift on only the left side of your face

OR

inject your eyelids with two pounds of collagen?

Things to consider: looking/talking like Rocky

Would you rather...

have a migrating mole beauty mark that wanders all over your face

OR

have 8-balls for pupils?

Would you rather...

be limited to wearing Tevas and socks for footwear

OR

only be able to use a plastic Walgreen's bag as a purse or wallet?

YOU MUST CHOOSE!

Would you rather...

have noses protruding from all over your body

OR

have 6 foot long armpit hair?

Would you rather...

all your weight go to your thighs **OR** to your butt?

to your stomach **OR** to your ankles and upper arms?

to your neck **OR** to your forehead?

YOU MUST CHOOSE!

Would you rather...

have perpetual camel toe

OR

perpetual muffin-top?

Would you rather...

be limited to a half pound of clothing every day

OR

have to wear no less than 30 pounds of jewelry?

Things to consider: exercising at the gym, cold days

Would you rather...

have broccoli for hair **OR** pins for facial hair?

ladles for hands **OR** large dreidels for feet?

a live sparrow for a belly button **OR** pumpkins for testicles?

YOU MUST CHOOSE!

Would you rather...

be on *Project Runway*

OR

have your significant other go on *What Not to Wear?*

Would you rather...

have eyelashes that connect from one eye to the other

OR

nose hair that connects from one nostril to the other?

Would you rather...

receive every haircut from a non-English speaking stylist at Supercuts

OR

have your wardrobe consist exclusively of Dress Barn hand-me-downs?

YOU MUST CHOOSE!

Would you rather...

have copious amounts of areola hair

OR

a "happy trail" that reached your neck?

Would you rather...

have to wear a four pound nipple piercing

OR

have a four-inch radius genital hoop ring?

Would you...

pay an additional 20% income tax for the rest of your life if you could give all your weight-gain to another person of your choosing?

YOU MUST CHOOSE!

SPA MENU

The Deity invites you to enjoy a spa weekend. He hands you an itinerary and firmly reminds you the choices are mandatory.

Would you rather take...

a sewage mudbath

OR

a human sweat Jacuzzi?

Would you rather...

get a whale sperm facial

OR

Magic Shell microdermabrasion?

YOU MUST CHOOSE!

Would you rather...

have to wear live spider earrings

OR

used tampon earrings?

Would you rather...

have to always go shopping and try on clothes with your mother

OR

have to go shopping and try on clothes with an invective-spitting Stacy and Clinton from *What Not To Wear?*

Would you rather...

always wear a top that left two holes for your nipples

OR

a pair of spandex with an ambiguous misshapen bulge at your crotch?

YOU MUST CHOOSE!

Would you rather...

have your arms come out of your head

OR

come out of your knees?

Would you rather...

have a barely formed second head of Bob Barker sprouting from the side of your own head

OR

have your head permanently turned 45 degrees?

Would you rather...

have a goatee around each eye

OR

earlobes that connected under your chin?

YOU MUST CHOOSE!

Would you rather...

have extra eyeballs in the palms of your hands

OR

have hair that styles itself?

Would you rather...

the current fashion trend be high-waisted jeans

OR

low-waisted?

Would you rather...

only wear clothes on the left side of your body

OR

only on the bottom half?

YOU MUST CHOOSE!

Would you rather...

shave your pubic area in a question mark

OR

exclamation mark?

Things to consider: Which one symbolizes that area better?

Would you rather always have to wear...

suspenders adorned with no less than 15 pieces of flair **OR** a tiara?

a marching band's drum on your shoulders **OR** orthodontic headgear?

a solid gold grill over your teeth **OR** 14 tubes of lipstick (you can use it wherever as long as it is exposed)?

Would you rather...

have to heavily bedazzle every article of clothing you own

OR

whenever outside, have to wear sunglasses in which each lens is as large as your head?

YOU MUST CHOOSE!

Would you rather...

have tempura-battered nipples

OR

produce caramel under your arms when sweating?

Would you rather...

have the physique of Gollum from *Lord of the Rings*

OR

Fat Albert?

Would you rather...

have the neck of a 90 year-old

OR

have the feet of a 90 year-old?

YOU MUST CHOOSE!

Would you rather...

have perpetually lit candle wicks at the end of each finger

OR

have sixteen-knuckled fingers?

Would you rather...

have to wear a nose ring that is connected to an earring with only a two inch chain

OR

have to wear a lip ring connected to a belly button ring with a twelve inch chain?

Would you rather...

have to wear three layers of sweats whenever you go to the beach

OR

wear Borat's neon green stretchy one-piece bathing suit whenever you go to the beach?

YOU MUST CHOOSE!

Would you rather...
have cellulite over 100% of your body

OR

have smooth skin but weigh 300 pounds?

Would you rather...
have Meg Ryan's cosmetic surgeon

OR

Kenny Rogers' cosmetic surgeon?

Would you rather...
gain 30 pounds

OR

three pounds all in your face?

YOU MUST CHOOSE!

Would you rather...

wear cologne scented as hot tar

OR

fish taco?

Would you rather...

have your eyes and big toes switch places

OR

your nose and belly button?

YOU MUST CHOOSE!

Would you rather always have to wear...

knee pads **OR** elbow pads?

an Eskimo coat **OR** a T-shirt that says "Makin' Bacon" along with a picture of two pigs humping?

a salami eye patch **OR** a lettuce yarmulke?

Would you rather...

have razor burn that forms treasure maps

OR

acne that spells out Braille love poetry?
Things to consider: marrying a blind person

Would you rather...

drool creamed spinach

OR

lactate Tang?

YOU MUST CHOOSE!

EXTREME BEAUTY, BODY, APPEARANCE AND FASHION

Would you rather...

have stretch marks all over your face

OR

have a pimento in each ear?

Would you rather...

have Patrick Ewing's arms on your body

OR

Patrick Ewing's nose on your face?

Would you rather...

have constantly wriggling body hair

OR

have a mustache that is constantly doing the wave?

YOU MUST CHOOSE!

291

Would you rather...

have a head that is half normal size

OR

twice normal size?

Would you rather...

fart the smell of lavender

OR

belch the sound of church bells in the distance?

Would you rather...

allow your mom to pick a tattoo for you

OR

allow your sibling?

YOU MUST CHOOSE!

Would you rather wear clothes made of...

balsa wood **OR** Fruit Roll-Up?

bamboo **OR** tin foil?

old '80s album covers **OR** Cap'n Crunch boxes?

Would you rather...

have nostrils that are constantly blowing out air

OR

a navel that is constantly sucking in air?

YOU MUST CHOOSE!

Authors' Debate

Let me proceed — Justin Heimberg

All it takes is some smart attentive constant grooming, and you'll look perfectly normal. If you're feeling lazy, you can just let it grow and swoosh it to the side like that Blagojevich guy. You can even cultivate the Travolta-like widow's peak with some artful shaving. A receding hairline gives you no choice other than go bald or a front-comb, the most perverse of the comb-over's incarnations. There's no freedom in that. In today's economy, you need to be recession-proof.

Let me recede — David Gomberg

Thanks to Michael Jordan, baldness became an acceptable even chic hairstyle—for black people in the '80s, and for white people a short fifteen years later. You can always shave your head close when it becomes too thin and scraggly. And you know where you're headed with male pattern baldness. But where does the hair procession stop? Does it sneak down your nose, over your lips, dribbling down your chin and neck, extending into a hairy isthmus[1] merging with your pubes? And yes, you can shave this torrent of hair, but then you need to deal with forehead stubble, which while a great band name, is a hideous and grotesque image.

1 And A Happy New Year!

EXTREME BEAUTY, BODY, APPEARANCE AND FASHION

13

Extremely Personal

It's time to get personal. How personal? We'll give you a hint. It rhymes with "blexcreamley". It's not hard. Just personalize WYR by taking the everyday people in your life and placing them in the following extreme situations.

Would you rather...

give a feverish lap dance to _____

(insert friend's mom)

OR

get a feverish lap dance from _____ ?

(insert another friend's mom)

Would you rather...

fight _____

(insert tough acquaintance)

OR

have sex with _____ ?

(insert gross acquaintance)

Would you...

passionately kiss _____ to have sex with _____ ?

(insert relative)   (insert someone hot)

YOU MUST CHOOSE!

Would you rather...

have the person on your left's hair

OR

the person on your right's butt?

Would you rather...

bump, grind, freak, and otherwise dirty dance
with _____
            (insert friend's mom or teacher or someone else inappropriate)

OR

pose naked for _____?
                   (insert magazine)

Would you rather...

forcefully punch _____ in the _____
           (insert relative)   (insert body part)

OR

smother and kill _____?
           (insert pet)

YOU MUST CHOOSE!

Would you rather...

have _____ 's body
(insert fit friend)
OR

_____ 's intelligence?
(insert smart friend)

Would you rather...

have a threesome with _____
(insert attractive acquaintance)
and _____
(insert unattractive acquaintance)
OR

have a threesome with _____ ?
(insert two average looking acquaintances)

Would you rather...

be Siamese twins with _____
(insert disgusting acquaintance)
OR

_____ ?
(insert annoying acquaintance)

YOU MUST CHOOSE!

Would you rather...

have a Real Doll of _____
(insert someone you know)

OR

a voodoo doll of _____ ?
(insert someone you dislike)

Would you rather...

have _____ 's clothes
(insert unstylish person)

OR

_____ 's imagination?
(insert boring person)

Would you rather...

grope _____
(insert hot person)

OR

have sex with _____ ?
(insert average looking person)

YOU MUST CHOOSE!

Would you rather...

fight in the octagon _____
(insert bad-ass acquaintance)

OR

four _____ s?
(insert wimpy acquaintance)

Would you rather...

be stuck on a desert island with your parents

OR

_____ ?
(insert somewhat unappealing person)

Would you rather...

fart wetly and loudly in front of _____
(insert relative)

OR

_____ ?
(insert someone you have a crush on or are trying to impress)

Would you rather...

club _____
(insert baby animal)

OR

go clubbing with _____ ?
(insert worst person you know)

YOU MUST CHOOSE!

Would you rather...

take a clean punch to the jaw by _____

(insert strong friend)

OR

spend a sixteen hour car ride with _____ ?

(insert annoying person)

Would you rather...

have _____ 's nose

(insert someone you are with)

OR

_____ 's body?

(insert someone else you are with)

Would you rather...

believe in the philosophical views of _____

(insert philosopher)

OR

_____ ?

(insert five year-old you know)

YOU MUST CHOOSE!

Would you rather...

take off your clothes, squat, and make a number two
in front of _____
(insert friend's parents)

OR

put a mask on, sneak up, and put a sleeper hold
on _____ ?
(insert friend's mom)

If your life depended on it, would you rather...

have _____ as your tennis partner
(insert uncoordinated friend)

OR

_____ as your your lifeline on *Who Wants to*
(insert dumb acquaintance)

be a Millionaire?

Would you rather...

have your genitals located on your _____
(insert body part)

OR

your _____ ?
(insert another body part)

YOU MUST CHOOSE!

Would you rather...

have to mutually masturbate with _____
(insert inappropriate acquaintance)

OR

go down on _____?
(insert unhygienic person)

Would you rather...

make pancakes with _____
(insert random person)

OR

play Wiffleball with _____?
(insert another random person)

Would you rather...

drop your pants and moon _____
(insert relative)

OR

give a hickey to _____?
(insert disgusting person)

YOU MUST CHOOSE!

Would you rather...

spend one week handcuffed to _____
(insert most shy acquaintance)

OR

_____ ?
(insert most garrulous acquaintance)

Would you rather...

cc _____ on all of your emails for a week
(insert someone else's parents)

OR

have _____ have access to your Internet browser history?
(insert dignified acquaintance)

Would you rather...

suck the toes of _____
(insert most vile acquaintance)

OR

vigorously tongue the armpits of _____ ?
(insert least hygienic friend)

YOU MUST CHOOSE!

Would you rather...

push _____ in front of a moving vehicle
(insert close friend)

OR

play one round of Russian roulette with _____ ?
(insert member of immediate family)

Would you rather...

manually stimulate _____
(insert close friend's father)

OR

have a three-way with _____ while _____
(insert close friend's parents)   *(insert the ghost of a historical figure)*
watched?

Would you rather...

have nightly sex with _____ for a week
(insert unattractive person)

OR

for the same week, be the official "wiper"
of _____ ?
(insert person you know with worst stomach issues)

YOU MUST CHOOSE!

Would you...

Simple yes or no questions aren't always so simple. For example, "Examined within a framework of dialectal materialism, was Marx right when he professed that those who control the means of production inevitably usurp power from the bourgeois?" Luckily for you, only a few of the following "Would you...?" questions concern dialectical materialism, and even those in some way tend to involve farting.

Would you...

spend two weeks wearing nothing but a g-string and Tevas for $20,000?

Would you...

sit in the bleachers and heckle the outfielders at a Special Olympics softball game for an inning for $13,000?

Would you...

take the surname of your spouse upon marriage (they were adamant about it) if it were "Chode"? "Doodition"? Cheeksqueakers?"

Would you...

pay $10,000 a year for a personal blues musician who magically appears to give harmonica accompaniment when you start complaining?

YOU MUST CHOOSE!

Would you...

masturbate only to *National Geographic* for the rest of your life for $500,000?

Would you...

change your name to "Blelko McGubbern" for $200,000?

Would you...

anonymously, wearing a mask, kick your grandma in the stomach for $100,000?

Then would you knee her jaw for $600,000?

Then spear her to the ground for $300,000?

Then blow a snot-rocket on her for $75,000?

Then drop a big elbow on her for $200,000 – totaling $1,275,000?

YOU MUST CHOOSE!

Would you...

accept the power to be able to fly in exchange for weighing 500 pounds?

Would you...

attempt to hold in your bowel movements for two weeks for $50,000 if and only if you succeed?

Would you...

have your nose surgically altered so that you have one giant nostril for $3,000,000?

YOU MUST CHOOSE!

If you never got caught, would you...

cheat on your partner with your choice of George Clooney or Jessica Alba?

If you never got caught, would you...

cheat on your partner with your choice all of the Victoria's Secret models at once or your top five rock stars?

YOU MUST CHOOSE!

For $300,000 deposited in your bank account today, would you name your kid...

Scrotie?

Rommel?

Neldar 9?

DeJustin?

Porp-Porp?

The sound of a bus door opening?

Would you...

wear a monocle to your job for a day for $500?

YOU MUST CHOOSE!

Would you...

if the Deity made it possible, have a third nipple for $100,000?
At $100,000 a nipple, how many would you have?

Would you, if there were no consequences...

slap Paula Abdul in the face?

Would you, if there were no consequences...

punch Donald Trump in the face?

YOU MUST CHOOSE!

Would you...
adopt your partner's hairstyle for $25,000 a year as long as you kept it?

Would you...
have sex with a baby harp seal to have sex with all the Playmates of the current year (men); with *People's 50 Sexiest Men* (women)?

Would you...
attempt to remove your own appendix with a pocket knife and some rubbing alcohol for $5,000,000?

Would you...
step in front of an 8 year-old to catch a foul ball at a baseball game if you knew you'd catch it?

YOU MUST CHOOSE!

Winner takes home $1,000,000, and the fight is to the Death.

Would you fight...

two emus?

Prince, if he had a knife?

600 tortoises?

a samurai who is on his cell phone possibly breaking up with his girlfriend?

1,000 possessed paper clips?

Would you...

permanently lose ten IQ points if you lost ten pounds permanently?

YOU MUST CHOOSE!

Would you...

wear swim goggles all week for $1,000?
Make it happen.

Would you...

sit on a bowl of green beans for an hour for $120 dollars?
Make it happen.

Would you...

want your partner to permanently lose ten IQ points if they lost
ten pounds permanently?

Would you...

offer advertising on your gravestone if it gave those mentioned
in your will $1,000 a month increasing at the rate of inflation?

YOU MUST CHOOSE!

Would you...

stoop to using the homeless holding signs advertising your business if you could pay them only a dollar a day?

Would you...

put product placement in your every day dialogue (have to mention, say, Kellogg's cereals at least 40 times a day in your every day conversations) for $100 a day? Example: "The day is as nice as Special K is crunchy! How are the kids?"

Would you...

want to have sex with Jennifer Lopez if she gained 50 pounds? 80? 100? 200?

Would you...

want to have sex with Johnny Depp if he gained 50 pounds? 100? 200?

YOU MUST CHOOSE!

Would you...

for $3,000, go to a junior high school, wait outside, and then when a nerdy kid walks out, walk past him and knock his books down in front of everybody, then walk away, never to be seen again?

Would you...

blog about your relationship life for $1,000 a week?

Would you...

pay $2,000 a year for a personal clothes shopper for your partner?

Would you...

fight a retarded cougar to the death if the winner gets $1,000,000?

YOU MUST CHOOSE!

Would you...

have sex with Leonard DiCaprio (women)/Shakira (men) if he/she had no teeth? No teeth and no hair? No teeth, no hair, no knees, and an incurable case of the hiccups?

Would you...

type left-handed for the rest of your life if you could have unlimited sex with any porn star you wanted? Would you type with your tongue for the rest of your life? With your genitals?

Would you...

lose a finger to have sex with your choice of Halle Berry or Tom Brady? A thumb? A hand? An arm? A leg?

Would you...

have a sex change operation for $20,000,000?

YOU MUST CHOOSE!

Would you...

limit your attire to various matador outfits for $500,000?

Would you...

put your penis in a glory hole for $60,000 if you were told there was an equal chance of your mother, Jenna Jameson, and Greg Gumbel being on the other side?

Would you...

watch a porno movie starring your parents for $1,000? $10,000? $100,000? What's your price?

Would you...

watch a porno movie with your parents for $1,000? $10,000? $100,000?

YOU MUST CHOOSE!

Which of the following would you have sex with for your choice of $200,000 or the chance to have sex with your "top five" selections for the people in the world you most want to have sex with?

A sheep?

A cow?

An armadillo?

A rhino?

A Winnie the Pooh hand puppet?

A baboon?

A pack of Ewoks?

YOU MUST CHOOSE!

Would you...

have sex with a creature that was half Lucy Liu/half horse?
Which half would you want as the lower half and which as the upper?

Would you slyly masturbate to the point of orgasm...

On a public bus for $5,000?

At a Quizno's for $7,000

At your desk at work during working hours for $10,000?

At church for $200,000?

YOU MUST CHOOSE!

Would you...

become a crack addict for one year if you were given $5,000,000 one month into your addiction? What if you were given the money after you completed your year?

Would you...

be defenestrated from a second story window for $8,000?

Would you...

be fenestrated into a first story window for $50?

Wludo ouy...

eb ldixscde orf ?005,00$.

YOU MUST CHOOSE!

EXTRA EXTREMELY EXTREME EXTRAS:

Would You Rather...?'s *MindF*cks*: 9 Things To Do in Airports to Screw with People's Heads

① Happily walk toward the metal detector. Scream in agony and convulse as you pass through it. Shoot a fearful look to the person behind you before hurrying off in a glazed shock.

② Get in a quick workout by running the opposite way on moving sidewalk. Wear a headband and spandex.

③ Bring individual grocery items including vegetables, deli meat, and hygiene products, and place them on the x-ray conveyor belt. Have your check book and supermarket club card out and ready.

④ Wrap a luggage tag around your wrist and ride the baggage carousel motionless.

⑤ Try to check in your luggage: a) one marble b) a horseshoe crab with a red ribbon around it c) an 8" by 10" photo of Konstantin Chernenko.

YOU MUST CHOOSE!

⑥ Fill Sudoku grids in the Air Flight magazine with the number 6 over and over.

⑦ At arrival area, hold up a sign that says Zarkon, Galactic Time Traveler of the Year 3000. Wear a silver foil vest and matching arm bands.

⑧ At metal detector, along with your keys and coins, put the following in trays: a dozen condoms, Mapquest directions to a church, and anal beads.

⑨ Check a Commodore 64 instead of a laptop through the carry-on x-ray.

YOU MUST CHOOSE!

Extremely Random

Before it was co-opted by the masses, *Would You Rather…?* was originally concocted for fans of "random" humor. In the spirit of the extreme, we venture back to our random roots. Be forewarned: you'll either love or hate this chapter. Or both. (Please send all love and/or hate mail to random@sevenfooter.com.)

Would you rather live in a world where...

people aged to age forty then reversed the aging process to their birth/death

OR

people didn't die, they rather gradually turned into celery?

Would you rather...

sweat profusely between the hours of six pm and seven pm

OR

insistently think your name is Darryl during the month of February?

Would you rather...

be able to catalyze enthusiastic low-fives from everybody you meet

OR

have a sixth sense which makes you tingle when in the presence of mechanical engineers?

YOU MUST CHOOSE!

Would you rather...

be able to multiply shinguards

OR

be able to correctly predict the date of any beaver's death?

Things to consider: See if you can come up with an even more useless power; email it to uselesspower@sevenfooter.com

Would you rather...

have a sarcastic echo that repeats whatever you say in a mocking inflection

OR

cast a shadow that's not your own, but rather that of Alfred Hitchcock?

Would you rather...

have a 200 IQ but have difficulty "using your words" like a two year-old

OR

have a darling figure but be morbidly obsessed with dandelions?

YOU MUST CHOOSE!

Would you rather…

have a literally contagious laugh that causes other people to laugh just like you

OR

be compelled to "spot" people and psych them up when they're picking luggage off the carousel at an airport?

Would you rather…

have to stick every piece of gum you ever chew somewhere on your body when you're done with it

OR

always be blowing your breath hard and making an intense grimacing face like a dude bench-pressing?

YOU MUST CHOOSE!

Would you rather...

look like this

OR

look like this?

YOU MUST CHOOSE!

Would You Rather...? for Beginners

Would you rather...

be wealthy and happy

OR

be poor and malnourished?

Would you rather...

have high attractive angular cheek bones

OR

have an extremely lazy eye and cleft lip?

Would you rather...

have a delicate grace about you

OR

limp badly and have a club foot?

YOU MUST CHOOSE!

Would you rather...

marry a beautiful kind person

OR

a hideous, moronic jerk who plays the flute often, loudly, and badly?

Would you rather...

fight a creature with the head of a tiger and the body
of an anaconda

OR

a creature with the head of a trout and the body of a wallet?

YOU MUST CHOOSE!

Would you rather...

be bitten by a mosquito every ten seconds

OR

be bitten by former NBA great Ralph Sampson every two hours?

Would you rather...

have the stock ticker tape thing scrolling through your eyes
(you can still see)

OR

vehemently displace all your anger on a shy, undeserving busboy
named Luis?

YOU MUST CHOOSE!

Would you rather...

be incredibly sensitive to people named Melvin but have a blurry right ear

OR

only need three hours sleep but be allergic to anything purple?

Would you rather...

have a nasal condition whereupon blowing your nose, the Mormon Tabernacle Choir's chorus of "Hallelujah" rings out

OR

have your first-born come out looking exactly like a miniature Tony Bennett?

Would you rather...

have the voice in your head sound like Andy Dick

OR

have your self-esteem dependent upon your proximity to a Long John Silver's?

YOU MUST CHOOSE!

Would you rather...

HAVE SWISS CHEESE LINENS

OR

WALL TO WALL
GROUND BEEF CARPET?

Would you rather...

have flounder for a tongue

OR

a spatula for your left foot?

Would you rather...

be moisturized to death

OR

starve to death in your shower, unable to circumvent the lather/rinse/repeat conundrum?

Would you rather live in a world...

where the traditional greeting was to roll up your shirt, slap your stomach repeatedly and bellow "Baboosk!"

OR

where celebrities offered stool samples instead of autographs?

YOU MUST CHOOSE!

Would you lather...

(What began as a Japanese man's mispronunciation
became a game unto itself)

Would you lather... a Rottweiler?

Would you lather... Pat Sajak?

Would you lather... your naked self on national
TV for $50,000?

Would you lather... John Stamos's head circa 1985?

Would you rather...

have your sole pick-up line be "The Higgs Field is a theoretical superforce that permeates the universe endowing matter with mass"

OR

be forced to use only one perfume/cologne scent: bacon and herb?

Would you rather...

be reincarnated as an incontinent spaniel

OR

a bipolar frog?

Would you rather...

on Thursdays, become convinced that everybody's name is Stottlemeyer

OR

have an irresistible temptation to defecate in people's grandfather clocks?

YOU MUST CHOOSE!

Would you rather...

have a consistent long-range jumper but laugh hysterically at the sight of cream cheese?

OR

be extremely well-spoken but turn into McDonald's Grimace when the moon is full?

Would you rather...

bloppers dalst nork serstel rackel endo melp azoo

OR

ferden rappo lacas delden sasty moln, restee eisenclost zand?
Things to consider: Norbins, rastor clousers.

Would you rather...

have blood that smells like vanilla extract but have one of Mussolini's speeches boom from your hand whenever it was opened

OR

have perfect diction but compulsively hoard radishes, fondling them and giggling maniacally in their presence?

YOU MUST CHOOSE!

Would you rather...

BE AN EXPERT WHITTLER BUT HAVE A HEAD OF LETTUCE PERPETUALLY ORBITING YOU

"ELI WHITNEY PATENTED THE COTTON GIN ON MARCH 14, 1794!"

OR

BE ABLE TO BAKE SUCCULENT BROWNIES BUT HAVE A VARIETY OF TOURETTE'S SYNDROME WHERE YOU RANDOMLY EXCLAIM FACTS ABOUT ELI WHITNEY?

Would you rather...

have these stats:

Str: 18

Dex: 17

Con: 4

Int: 5

Wis: 4

Cha: 17

OR

these:

Str: 5

Dex: 4

Con: 18

Int: 17

Wis: 18

Cha: 4?

YOU MUST CHOOSE!

Would you rather be unable to distinguish between...

your shoes and milk cartons **OR** swabs and your keys?

the phrase "I love you" and the phrase "Pass the salt" **OR** the phrases "How are you?" and "I will destroy you!"?

the concept of reciprocity and coon-skin hats **OR** water and ballet?

Would you rather...

have extraordinary balance but have to wear a retainer the rest of your life

OR

have nifty word-smithing talent but have a pathological phobia of cummerbunds?

YOU MUST CHOOSE!

Would you rather...

have a dominating net game in tennis but be incapable
of recognizing the numeral 4

OR

be able to calculate exact postage for a letter/package by sight
but always have to keep your pubic hair gelled in Jheri curl style?

Would you rather...

be the spitting image of Sidney Poitier, but have calves as thick
as your waist

OR

be unbeatable when you throw first in backgammon,
but have frictionless soles on your feet?

Would you rather...

have your tongue and roof of your mouth coated in opposing sides of
Velcro

OR

your genitals and inner thighs?

YOU MUST CHOOSE!

The World's Worst Would You Rather...?'s

Would you rather...

jump on a grenade to save your friends and family

OR

just kind of slowly cover up the grenade?

Would you rather...

there was a silent "b" in "felt"

OR

the word "flounder" was spelled "pilfcone"?

Would you rather...

have the bunion of Paul Simon

OR

the Simon of Paul Bunyan (work in progress)?

YOU MUST CHOOSE!

Would you rather...

have the navigational instincts of Amerigo Vespucci but subsist on a diet of pet food

OR

be able to shine shoes with your gaze but have to make love to a croissant on a daily basis?

YOU MUST CHOOSE!

Would you rather...

have to walk single file with your friends whenever you went anywhere, have your dreams directed by the guy who directed Pan's Labyrinth, be able to enter the water without making a splash, but uncontrollably exclaim names of the various members of the Continental Congress during sexual climax

OR

have literal cauliflower ear, have a herring for a left hand, have to name your child Aesop, constantly be framing shots with your hands like a director, turn guys named Mervin yellow, and be able to spit pools that show visions of the future for a peasant in Laos?

YOU MUST CHOOSE!

Would you rather...

have a cork back, a comb-over beard, lust after Puss in Boots, have Wes Unseld's shadow, play daily *Arkanoid* games with Tony Randall, have to *register for your wedding* at Spencers Gifts and have *basil-scented farts*

OR have *butter-soaked skin, a maple scone for a foot*, get 5 o'clock *shadow all over your body*, have a *vast coaster* collection, have *Carl Weathers* borrow your pen and never *give it back*, and have a bulimia that causes you to *want to throw* up in mail *slots?*

YOU MUST CHOOSE!

Would you rather...

sneeze the sound of thunder

OR

pee pure energy?

YOU MUST CHOOSE!

Sexually Extreme

Because one sex chapter wouldn't be extreme enough...

If your life depended on it, would you rather have to have sex to the point of orgasm...

while staying on a running treadmill **OR** staying on a unicycle without falling off?

on a pogo stick **OR** on a seesaw without either end hitting the ground?

on an exercise ball without falling off **OR** sitting on a George Foreman Grill enduring the pain?

Would you rather...

have bland unspectacular sex with Antonio Banderas

OR

wild, passionate, freaky sex with Greg Gumbel?

YOU MUST CHOOSE!

Would you rather...

have bland unspectacular sex with Jessica Biel

OR

wild, passionate, freaky sex with Condoleezza Rice?

Would you rather be seduced by...

food **OR** music?

poetry **OR** massage?

origami **OR** shadow puppets?

Would you rather...

when getting too into it during sex, "tilt" like a pinball machine and stop functioning for a while

OR

be transported to Des Moines every time you orgasm?

YOU MUST CHOOSE!

Would you rather...

have to wear noise-proof headphones during sex

OR

a full leg cast?

Would you rather...

have sex with someone with problem flatulence

OR

with someone who has a life-size portrait tattoo of your uncle on their back?

Would you rather...

have to talk during sex in baby talk

OR

in beatnik slang from the '60s?

YOU MUST CHOOSE!

Would you rather...

have sex with Abu from *Aladdin*

OR

Flounder from the *Little Mermaid*?

Would you rather...

have a variety of conjunctivitis of the eye which, during sex, causes your partner to intermittently appear as Mao Tse Tung

OR

have to conduct all sexual activity in a pile of mulch?

Would you rather...

have a *Star Trek*–themed wedding **OR** a *Batman*–themed one?

an Ewok–themed wedding **OR** an *A-Team*–themed one?

a robot–themed wedding **OR** a Paul Bunyan–themed one?

YOU MUST CHOOSE!

Would you rather...

have your Facebook status update automatically report all specific sexual activity as you partake to the last detail

OR

have your Facebook profile display a complete group of people you've hooked up with?

Would you rather...

only be able to sleep with your best friend's sloppy seconds

OR

have to get your mother's written approval before sleeping with anyone?

Would you rather...

have a threesome with Colin Farrell and Artie Lang

OR

Matt Lauer and Bob Sagat?

YOU MUST CHOOSE!

Would you rather...

have a threesome with Gisele Bündchen and Rosie O'Donnell

OR

with two average looking women?

Would you rather...

have sex in an airplane bathroom

OR

on a golf course at night?

Would you rather...

have a magic screensaver that anticipates when someone
is coming into the room and automatically closes pornography

OR

a magic screensaver that shows you whatever Charlie Rose
is doing at the time?

YOU MUST CHOOSE!

Would you rather...

have your mom look at your current Internet browsing history

OR

at all of your last month's emails to your significant other?

Would you rather only be able to have sex...

missionary **OR** doggie-style?

oral sex **OR** intercourse?

performing a 69 **OR** 37?

Would you rather...

tell your partner everything about your sexual past

OR

tell them every sexual thought you have about another person?

YOU MUST CHOOSE!

Would you rather use as a sex toy...

a menorah **OR** a slab of beef?

a backscratcher **OR** a Rubik's Snake?

a Wacky WallWalker **OR** a double cheeseburger?

You live with a roommate. You decide to use a blacklight to reveal hidden "stains."

Would you rather...

find stains all over your coffee mug

OR

all over a picture of you and your family?

YOU MUST CHOOSE!

Would you rather...

speak like a pirate during sex

OR

yodel upon orgasm?
Things to consider: asking to have your timbers shivered

Would you rather...

be a supervillain that can kill people's sex drive at any moment
with the perfect personalized mood-killing hologram

OR

a supervillain who can queef 4.5 richter scale earthquakes?

Would you rather...

have orgasms that feel like doing a whippet

OR

that feel like jumping into the ocean on a hot day?

YOU MUST CHOOSE!

Would you rather...

have sex with Pinocchio

OR

with your *choice* of *Snow White* dwarf?

If your life depended on it, would you rather...

have to bring yourself to orgasm while your mom leaves you a long rambling answering machine message

OR

while staring, eyelids held open, at a poster of an adorable kitten?

Would you rather...

have porn quality sex but porn quality conversation as well

OR

have romantic comedy quality sex and romantic comedy quality conversation?

YOU MUST CHOOSE!

Three-ways with
Celebrity Supercouple Fish

Would you rather have a three-way with...

Albacore (Jessica Alba and Corey Feldman) **OR** Katfish (Kat Von D and Laurence Fishburne)?

Sardean (Sarah Michelle Geller and Dean Cain) **OR** Halibut (Halle Berry and Boutros Boutros-Ghali – alternative name Boutros Boutros Halle)?

Moray (Demi Moore and Ray Romano) **OR** Portmanteau (Natalie Portman and Tony Danza)?

YOU MUST CHOOSE!

Would you rather...

watch your parents having sex

OR

watch your grandparents having sex?

Would you rather...

be unable to shake the sporadic image of Gene Shalit
during sexual congress

OR

have pubic hair that grows whenever you're lying?

Would you rather...

have asparagus for nipples

OR

have a unique venereal disease where anytime you kiss someone you
briefly turn into an 1800s gold prospector, who is dead-set on the
finding that next big strike?

YOU MUST CHOOSE!

Would you rather...

be unable to perform sexually unless dressed up as a Spanish conquistador

OR

when attempting to shout out your partner's name when having sex, always instead yell "Stombin 6!"?

Would you rather...

have to wear foam "Number 1" hands when having sex

OR

have to wear loafers without socks?

Would you rather...

have sex with Yao Ming

OR

Orville Redenbacher?

YOU MUST CHOOSE!

Would you rather...

have genitalia that permanently reduces in size five percent each time it is used

OR

genitalia that multiplies after fifty uses?

Would you rather...

have your libido vary directly with the stock market

OR

have the sexual outcome of your dates be contingent on what base you reach, if any, via a roll of dice in Strat-O-Matic baseball?

Would you rather...

have one of your sexual encounters webcast

OR

appear in a *Zagat*-style guide based on submissions from your various sexual partners?

Things to consider: a "bumbling novice" who "couldn't find a clitoris with a divining rod" offers "mildly pleasant groping" and is "over in a flash."

YOU MUST CHOOSE!

Pick Your Penis

Would you rather...

have a penis that beeped like a Geiger counter the closer you get to a partner willing to put out

OR

have a penis that dispensed freshly brewed coffee?

Would you rather...

have a penis the consistency of bamboo

OR

the consistency of one of those water-filled things—I think it was called a snake—y'know, that rubber thing... you'd like squeeze it, and it'd squirm, that thing! From the eighties, you know what I'm talking about?

YOU MUST CHOOSE!

Would you rather...

have a clitoris that doubled as the on/off button for your television
OR
have a "mood clitoris" that changed color depending on your emotional state?

Would you rather...

only be able to sleep with sexual partners over the height of 7' **OR** under the height of 4'?

partners weighing over 500 lbs **OR** under 70 lbs?

partners whose names have exactly 11 letters **OR** partners born in Wyoming?

YOU MUST CHOOSE!

Would you...

dunk your scrotal sack in a pot of boiling water for ten seconds for $50,000?

Would you rather...

only be able to get turned on when your partner is dressed like Thurgood Marshall

OR

by listening to Shaquille O'Neal's album *Shaq-Fu: Da Return?*

Would you rather...

be completely incapable of moving when sexually attracted to someone

OR

mentally revert to yourself as 4 year-old whenever you are about to have any sort of sexual contact?

YOU MUST CHOOSE!

During sex, would you rather your partner say...

"I love you!" **OR** "F**k me!"?

"You're the greatest!" **OR** "Give it to me!"?

"Eisenhower shall return!" **OR** "The overlord shall be pleased!"?

Would you rather...

give birth to a baby with fully developed private parts

OR

with wings instead of arms?

Would you rather...

have your dirty talk dubbed with clean sound-alike words
(eg. "Fork that pony!"; "Sick that dog!")

OR

ejaculate Clearasil?

YOU MUST CHOOSE!

Would you rather have...

phone sex **OR** cybersex?

Telegraph sex **OR** Pictionary sex?

Morse code sex **OR** snail mail sex?

Would you rather...

be the world's greatest lover but marry your high school sweetheart at age 18

OR

have the talents of Shakespeare but be restricted to writing for *Penthouse Forum*?

Would you rather...

like big butts and be unable to fabricate about such matters

OR

find out your girlfriend is a centerfold, causing your blood temperature to starkly plummet?

YOU MUST CHOOSE!

Would you rather...

have sex with Kathy Griffin

OR

with Jessica Simpson in a bed of rusty nails?

Would you rather...

have a commemorative chess set made from your various sexual partners

OR

have Ken Burns make a nine part documentary about your sex life?

Would you rather...

always be drunk during sex

OR

never be drunk during sex?

YOU MUST CHOOSE!

Would you rather...

have sex on bed sheets depicting bloody scenes from wars

OR

sheets with smiling pictures of your parents?

Would you rather...

have to list your penis size/breast size on your business card

OR

have to use the email for all business and pleasure:
hobbitpumper@gmail.com?

Would you rather...

use a Netflix system for condoms

OR

toilet paper?

YOU MUST CHOOSE!

Would you rather...

have a penis of ever-changing girth

OR

have balls of ever-changing weight?

Would you rather...

have an ass crack that is 2/3 the way to the left of your body

OR

have an ass crack that extends up to and between your shoulder blades?

Would you rather...

only be able to communicate during romance and sex through facial expression

OR

text message?

YOU MUST CHOOSE!

EXTRA EXTREMELY EXTREME

Now we are talking. Even yelling a bit. We have traversed the realm of the slightly extreme, skipped right over the somewhat extreme into the dangerous territory of the fairly extreme. And now we find ourselves in the terrifying, tantalizing, titillating redundant world of the Extra Extremely Extreme. Put on your safety vest and special person's pads, and get ready to push it … to the extremely extreme! Extra-ly!

Would you rather live in a world where...

babies had mute buttons

OR

where parents did?

Would you rather...

belch the scent of roses

OR

fart smooth jazz?

Would you rather...

be eating a burrito and discover a long, long hair in your mouth

OR

be licking a Tootsie Pop, only to find a small human embryo in the middle?

YOU MUST CHOOSE!

Would you rather...

have a voice whose volume is permanently set at the equivalent of 8 on a stereo

OR

speak at ten times normal speed?
Things to consider: child-rearing, sex

Would you rather...

sleep nightly in pajamas made of dentists' used gauze

OR

have to reach into a horse's ass every time you want the key to your apartment?

Would you rather...

have a ballet based on your life

OR

have a melodramatic cheesy *90210*-like show based on your life?

YOU MUST CHOOSE!

Would you rather watch...

"The Mormon Bachelor"

30 hopeful beautiful single ladies compete, but only three to five will be chosen to be the wives of the... *The Mormon Bachelor*. Consider the intrigue when the Mormon Bachelor finds a girl he really likes but she doesn't get along with the other prospective spouses, threatening the cohesiveness of the unit.

OR

"Foreign or Retarded" (game show)?

Would you rather...

breathe to the tune of "Mr. Roboto"

OR

have your speech badly dubbed over like in a Japanese monster movie?

Would you rather...

be a Siamese octuplet

OR

have to raise octuplets?

Things to consider: hoping to be a "corner unit" in the octuplet chain, playing Red Rover

YOU MUST CHOOSE!

Would you rather live in a world where...

it is illegal for people under 18 to buy cigarettes

OR

where it is illegal for people over 40 to buy cigarettes?

Things to consider: Cigarette smoking starts to seriously affect your health if you smoke after 40, whereas smoking up to that point has little statistical effect on health. Why the hell do we ban them for young people when it would make a lot more sense in terms of social cost and societal health to ban smoking for older adults? Next caller.

Would you rather...

have genital warts

OR

eyeball zits?

Would you rather... (Jewish moms only)

have your daughter date a gentile man

OR

a Jewish woman?

YOU MUST CHOOSE!

Would you rather...

be twisted like a balloon animal

OR

be a human puck on a giant air hockey table of the gods?

Things to consider: How long it would take for you to die and how would it happen?

Would you rather...

only be able to eat garnish to survive

OR

only be able to drink human-lactated milk?

Would you rather...

have your fingernails peeled off, one by one

OR

your hair, head and body, pulled out one by one?

Would you rather...

speak like Martin Luther King with a horrible lisp

OR

like Jimmy Fallon in the middle of taking a dump?

YOU MUST CHOOSE!

Would You Rather...? Hobo Traits

Would you rather...

carry all your personals including a laptop in a hobo bag on a stick

OR

only be able to travel by freight train cars?

Would you rather...

have all kinds of crazy stunts happen to you like Charlie Chaplin's the *Little Tramp*

OR

not?

Would you rather...

have hobo charcoal marks on your face

OR

have a dreadful PTSD alcoholic, homeless lifestyle that is inaccurately romanticized by movies and popular culture?

YOU MUST CHOOSE!

Would you rather...

occasionally "lose reception" in face to face dialogue and be unable to hear what people are saying

OR

be compelled to dance like a stripper whenever you see a pole of any kind?

Would you rather...

have to keep a hard-boiled egg in your mouth at all times

OR

have to keep one in your ass at all times?

Would you rather live in...

a massive house of cards **OR** a house of mirrors?

a house of glass **OR** wicker?

a house of Nerf **OR** chocolate?

YOU MUST CHOOSE!

Would you rather...

grate all of your back skin off

OR

microwave your head for ten seconds?

Would you rather...

have to type forever with no vowels

OR

no hands?

Would you rather...

be able to decipher the handwriting of any doctor

OR

be able to generate angst in turtles?

YOU MUST CHOOSE!

Would you rather...

(pirates only) never be able to say "Aarrgh"

OR

have a sissy pink sequined eye patch?

Would you rather...

use gasoline as shampoo

OR

wipe yourself with extra-adhesive tape?

Would you rather...

have foldable Swiss army knife devices for fingernails

OR

have nunchucks for hair?

YOU MUST CHOOSE!

Would you rather go on a trip to...

Striking Baseball Fantasy Camp—Make lavish demands with real big leaguers! Sleep til noon and attend dive-bars and get drunk! These are just a few of the tantalizing childhood fantasies you can live out when you get to hang out with baseball players doing what they do best—striking!

OR

Vietnam War Reenactment Weekend—Relive history! Simulate jungle warfare, ingest Agent Orange, flip out and burn an innocent village to the ground, and shoot your own troops. Fun and educational!

Would you rather...

only be able to have sex on Tuesdays

OR

only during even minutes of the day (3:22, 3:24, 3:26, etc.)?

Would you rather...

be a chronic procrastinator

OR

(work in progress)?

YOU MUST CHOOSE!

Would You Rather...?'s Inside Jokes

Would you rather...

go shoe shopping with Larry

OR

tell Renaldo he is overreacting?

Things to consider: Larry's deliberation, Renaldo's temper

Would you rather...

have cow-sized nipples

OR

have all your dirty words and vulgar expressions censored with silly bleeps, buzzes, and cuckoos?

Would you rather...

have to walk with your feet never leaving the ground

OR

never be able to use the same word twice in any given 24-hour period?

Things to consider: Try both for a day.

YOU MUST CHOOSE!

Would you rather live in a world where...

scratching your crotch prevented cancer

OR

where the mythic figures of childhood fantasy were real? (i.e., the Tooth Fairy, Easter Bunny, Santa Clause, the Lord of Brisket.)

Would you rather...

have the hands of a 90 year-old

OR

the boobs of a 90 year-old?

Would you rather...

use your mouth to change a light bulb

OR

to flush a public toilet?

YOU MUST CHOOSE!

Would you rather play...

Fantasy Basketball - White Edition

Players choose exclusively white players from the NBA and score points for picks set, hustle baskets, scrapping for loose balls, "doing the intangibles", smart, heady play, unselfishness, moving well without the ball, etc.

OR

Magnetic Militant Black Poetry

Boasts magnetic tabs on which you'll find words like, "whitey", "die", "the Man", and "oppression". Sample poem: "the Man burns. Whitey Oppression." 300 magnetic tabs.

Would you rather...

only be able to use thermometers rectally

OR

be able to use thermometers by mouth but only ones that have been previously used rectally (you can rinse them)?

YOU MUST CHOOSE!

Would you rather...

BE A SIAMESE TWIN WITH YAO MING

OR

MINI-ME?

Would you rather...

only be able to sleep in trees **OR** under cars?

in airports **OR** hanging upside down like a bat?

at rock concerts **OR** on crabbing boats?

Would you rather...

pierce your cheek **OR** your knee?

your tongue **OR** your fingertip?

your uvula **OR** your perineum?

Would you rather...

have glow in the dark acne

OR

have caramel ear wax?

YOU MUST CHOOSE!

Would you rather...

have a chauffeur who is an insecure 15 year-old getting his learner's permit

OR

a chauffeur who is a 90 year-old grandmother?

Would you rather...

have to clean yourself like a cat

OR

take a dump in a box of litter like a cat?

Would you rather...

be a Siamese twin connected by the nose

OR

by the buttcheeks?

YOU MUST CHOOSE!

Would you rather...

communicate in the tone of a sappy Hallmark card

OR

in Def Comedy?

Would you rather...

hammer a nail through your hand

OR

use boiling water eye drops?

Would you rather...

defecate colorful and intricate kaleidoscope patterns

OR

urinate in solid rods?

YOU MUST CHOOSE!

Would you rather...

have to use an Amish hospital

OR

have your only source of education be the back of oatmeal packets?

Would you rather...

snore the sound of a trumpet

OR

with the power of a vacuum?

Would you rather...

have your bedroom designed like a prison cell

OR

like a giant version of a hamster cage?
Things to consider: cedar chips, exercise wheel

YOU MUST CHOOSE!

Would you rather...

do this connect the dots **OR** *this one?*

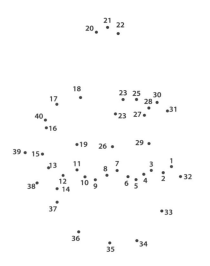

YOU MUST CHOOSE!

Would you rather...

be constantly followed by an environmentalist who loudly points out everything you do that's killing the environment

OR

be followed around by a personal trainer who loudly points out everything you do that's bad for yourself?

Would you rather...

have ears that face backwards

OR

eyes that blink sideways?

Would you rather...

date an otherwise hot person with bad cauliflower ear

OR

terrible turkey neck?

YOU MUST CHOOSE!

Would you rather...

have your rectum located in the palm of your hand

OR

on the bottom of your foot?

Would you rather...

have your heart located outside your chest

OR

have your skin and flesh stop short of your feet like Capri pants?

Would you rather...

be able to dispense salt and pepper out of your nostrils

OR

be able to fill in bubbles on multiple choice tests with enviable precision?

Would you rather...

be a dew drop on a tulip

OR

be a tear drop of joy?

YOU MUST CHOOSE!

Would you rather...

have a retractable ball-point pen in your finger

OR

have a laser pointer finger?

Would you rather...

have a sleep disorder that causes you to appear as Kim Jong-II
any time you lie down

OR

not be able to remember every other minute of your life?

Would you rather...

breathe through your navel

OR

your butt?
Things to consider: snorkeling

YOU MUST CHOOSE!

Would you rather...

get caught in a snowstorm of throwing stars

OR

a rainstorm of sulfuric acid?

Would you rather...

have sex with a 50% scale Brad Pitt

OR

a regular-sized Bob Costas?

Would you rather...

have sex with a 200% scale Shakira

OR

Kate Winslet?

YOU MUST CHOOSE!

Would you rather...

wear a three-cornered hat

OR

wear reverse heels where the toe is six inches higher than the heel?

Would you rather...

have a Nerf lawn

OR

have bean-bag bushes?

Would you rather...

purposely run over a squirrel

OR

slap a full-nelson on an elderly stranger for five minutes?

Would you rather...

have moving tattoos

OR

a tattoo that changed each day to an image that expressed how you are feeling?

YOU MUST CHOOSE!

ROADKILL:
FUN AND GAMES ON THE GO

ROADKILL CAR BINGO

Divide into two teams. Each team picks a Bingo page.
Each time you spot one of the items below, mark the box.

Person giving the finger	Someone singing to themselves in a car	Drunk person on street
Jaywalker	Doobie Brothers song on radio	Nose-picker
Asshole who cuts you off	Religious zealot bumper sticker	Roadkill—deer, fox, or pelican

Card 1

The first team to mark three boxes in a row, horizontally, vertically, or diagonally wins. Or if you're not into the whole competition thing, work together.

Obese person eating in car	Graffiti with a misspelling	Audible fart
Mustard	Guy driving who thinks he is cooler than he actually is	Fuzzy Dice
Vanity license plate with sexual content	Guilt	Roadkill—squirrel, possum, or Ewok

ROADKILL SNAP JUDGMENT

Look at a car ahead of you. Guess what the person will look like based on their car. Include race, age, and sex. Be specific. For example, if you see a Volvo up ahead, you might say, "a middle-aged mom who's lost any sense of her sexuality", while another passenger might say "a hipster with horn-rimmed glasses." If you see a low-rider, you could guess "a bad-ass vato gang member" or "a redneck teenager smoking." Speed up (safely), get next to the car and look (safely) and see who is closest. Repeat (safely). First one to five points wins (safely).

Authors are not responsible for bad or irresponsible driving.

BATTLE HAIKU ROADKILL

Here's how this works: Two people engage in Battle Haiku, where they insult each other à la Battle Rap. But instead of rap, use the lost art of Japanese Haiku poetry. The poems must insult the opponent in a good-natured way and follow a syllable pattern of 5-7-5. Invoking nature is encouraged. Examples follow.

You have ugly teeth
Smile looks like wilting lotus
Crapped on by hawk

Well, you are so fat
Flesh is like cumulus cloud
Drifting in the wind.

Damn, yo!

FACE OFF

Whoever is reading must convey the words below using charades. But here's the catch. You can only use your body from the neck up (i.e., your face).

- Disgusting
- Cross-eyed
- Drunk
- Horny
- Cunnilingus
- Pink Eye
- William H. Macy
- Supercilious

Team 1

408

See how many you can get in three minutes. If you'd like, split into teams. Each time you use a part of your body other than your face, deduct one point. Winner gets the next food stop paid for.

Team 2

- Excited
- Death
- Worry
- Gum
- Sexy
- Spit
- Vomit
- Vasco da Gama

ROADKILL TWO TRUTHS AND A LIE

Each person shares 3 one- or two-sentence stories about themselves, two of which are true. The, the others guess which is the lie.

Here's an example from the authors.

- A model dating a seven-footer was impressed with the use of seven-footers in our books and set Gomberg up on a date with another model.

- Two friends solicited Heimberg via email and he made a tour to "visit" each of them. They asked that they someday be mentioned in one of the books.

- Gomberg hooked up with a professional Cyndi Lauper look-alike.

To find our which is a lie, email: twotruthsonelie@sevenfooter.com

BELOW THE BELT

Whoever is reading must convey the words below using charades. But her's the catch. You can only use your body from the waist down. (Driver, keep your eyes on the road!)

- Baseball
- Pray
- Ejaculate
- Shake
- Athlete's Foot
- Poop
- Rocket
- Crabs
- Pendulum
- Croissant

Don't stop there. Have someone choose more words and whisper them to the actor.

ROADKILL MIND CONTROL

Each player or team reads an Objectives Page (and does not look at the other Objectives Page). Read the objectives to yourself, making sure that no one else sees them. Now, go about your business as you normally would, looking for opportunities to achieve your objectives.

MIND CONTROL OBJECTIVES PAGE 1

Get an opponent to:

- Retrieve an item from the garbage.

- Draw the "Peace" symbol.

- Unbutton a button on another person's clothing.

- Say "radish" and "milk" in the same sentence.

- Say "nice shot."

- Put on another person's glasses.

- Imitate a farm animal.

All of the objectives require you to get one of your opponents to do something. It can be any one of your opponents, and not all opponents must be present when the objective is achieved. After you successfully achieve an objective and verbally reveal it to your opponent(s), reward yourself one point. The game is over when a player successfully scores three points.

MIND CONTROL OBJECTIVES PAGE 2

Get an opponent to:

- Say "You're/You are an idiot."

- Give the "thumbs-down" sign.

- Sing a line from a Beatles song.

- Perform a push-up.

- Say "plum" and "asparagus" in the same sentence.

- Put his/her own finger in his/her own ear.

- Clap.

CHAPTER **19** NINETEEN

MORE WHO'D YOU RATHER...?

Across the animal kingdom, choosing an appropriate mate is vital to help ensure the survival of a species. Male humpback whales race in an array of flips and stunts so the female can select the mate with the strongest genes, while peacocks fan their magnificent tail feathers to show peahens who's got the most impressive plumed booty. For human beings, choosing a mate (whether it's for life or for a one night stand) is also a skill that must be honed. While the survival of the species may not be at stake, the survival of your self-respect, dignity, and disease-free genitals might be. With this in mind, we offer you the chance to sharpen your natural selection skills, by serving up these difficult dilemmas concerning possible partners. As always, you must choose. Abstinence is not an option.

Would you rather...

have sex with Heidi Montag

OR

Susan Boyle if you had to then listen to each of them sing
for six hours straight?

Would you rather...

have sex with Brad Pitt if he gained 150 pounds

OR

Jeff Foxworthy?

Would you rather...

do the Mac commercial guy and get $5000 worth of PC products

OR

do the PC guy and get $20,000 worth of Mac products?

YOU MUST CHOOSE!

Would you rather...

have sex with Kim Kardashian

OR

Ashley Olsen if they exchanged butts?

Would you rather have phone sex with...

Tracy Morgan **OR** Alex Trebek?

T-Pain **OR** Al Gore?

the banker from *Deal or No Deal* **OR** Oscar the Grouch?

YOU MUST CHOOSE!

Would you rather...

have phone sex with Alicia Keys **OR** Sarah Silverman?

Megan Fox after inhaling helium **OR** Chelsea Handler?

Tyra Banks **OR** JK Rowling?

a telemarketer who is trying to sell you something during the phone sex **OR** someone who subsequently requires you to answer a ten minute survey about your call?

Would you rather...

have a partner who will only give you oral sex if you do the "Vrrroooom! Here comes the airplane!" thing with your penis

OR

a partner who automatically shifts into an uncannily accurate Bill Cosby impression during all sexual activity?

Would you... have sex with Tyne Daly daily

to have sex with Keira Knightley, nightly?

YOU MUST CHOOSE!

It's All Relative

Would you rather...

for thirty seconds, make out with your mom

OR

with a hot curling iron?

Would you rather...

get a lap dance from your grandma

OR

give a lap dance to your grandma?

Things to consider: physical injury, psychological injury

Would you rather...

lewdly bump and grind with your grandfather to hip hop music

OR

give your uncle twenty neck hickeys?

YOU MUST CHOOSE!

Would you rather...

have sex with Spencer Pratt

OR

George Clooney if they exchanged personalities?

Would you rather...

have sex with a perfect 10 but get herpes

OR

have sex with a 2 and get a $10 coupon to Long John Silvers?

Would you rather...

have sex with Katie Couric

OR

Natalie Portman if she gained 100 pounds?

YOU MUST CHOOSE!

Would you rather...

have sex with a hot garbage man **OR** an unattractive rock star?

a porn star **OR** a pop star?

a hot dispassionate woman **OR** a down and dirty ugly woman with a unibrow and a goiter on her neck the size of a Dixie cup?

an incredibly witty sumo wrestler **OR** a mysterious and troubled busboy?

a barber shop quartet whose members make all sexual sounds and exclamations in harmony **OR** a pack of Ewoks?

YOU MUST CHOOSE!

Would you rather...

have snail mail sex (bawdy letters sent back and forth over a period of months)

OR

have sign language sex?
Things to consider: How would you pleasure yourself while signing?

Would you rather...

have sex with Siamese triplet Jessica Albas (male); Johnny Depps (female)

OR

with just the singular version?

Would you rather...

have sex with a man with a 1-inch penis

OR

a 17-inch penis? Oral sex?

Would you rather...

have sex with Rosie O'Donnell

OR

have to push her up a steep hill?

Would you rather...

have sex with Sarah Palin

OR

Tina Fey?

What if you had to talk to them for three hours before and after the sex?

Things to consider: The porn *Nailin' Palin* was made shortly after her vice-presidential bid. What other political porns can you think of that should be made? Examples: *Ridin' Biden, Bush!*

YOU MUST CHOOSE!

By the Numbers

Would you rather...

take it from Conchata Ferrell from *Two and a Half Men* wearing a 3" strap-on

OR

from Scarlett Johansson wearing a 10" strap-on?

Would you rather...

get a hand job from a perfect 10 **OR** have sex with a 6?

a foot job from an 8 **OR** have sex with a 5?

a knee job from a 2 **OR** have brunch with a 4?

YOU MUST CHOOSE!

Would you rather...

have sex with a Cyclops Angelina Jolie with the arms of a gorilla and the trunk of an elephant

OR

Joy Behar?

Would you rather...

have sex with Orlando Bloom **OR** Tom Brady?

Chris Daughtry **OR** LeBron James?

Robert Pattinson in character as Edward Cullen **OR** Robert Pattinson, the actor?

YOU MUST CHOOSE!

Would you rather...

give the person on your left a massage and "happy ending"

OR

give the person on your right a thorough prostate exam?

Would you rather...

tongue-kiss the person to your left

OR

get slapped by the person on your right?

YOU MUST CHOOSE!

Fun with Puppets

Would you rather...

have sex with Big Bird

OR

Cookie Monster?

Things to consider: CM's voracious appetite, contracting a Bird Flu STD

Would you rather...

have sex with The Count

OR

Snuffleupagus?

Things to consider: the Count's OCD, Snuffy produces 18 gallons of ejaculate upon orgasm

YOU MUST CHOOSE!

Robbin' The Cradle

Would you rather...

have sex with the offspring of Josh Duhamel and Fergie when it grows up **OR** the child of Katie Holmes and Tom Cruise?

the offspring of Gisele and Tom Brady **OR** of Angelina Jolie and Brad Pitt?

the offspring of Seal and Heidi Klum **OR** David and Victoria Beckham?

YOU MUST CHOOSE!

Would you rather...

have sex with an auctioneer who speaks in auctioneer inflection during sex

OR

an aspiring rapper who freestyle rhymes during sex?

Things to consider: Try both.

Would you rather...

have sex with the fourth image when you Google "swarthy"

OR

the third image when you Google "albino"?

Things to consider: Make your choice before Googling, then check and see what you are dealing with.

YOU MUST CHOOSE!

Would you rather...

have sex with Lady Gaga and then have to wear her outfits
for a month

OR

have sex with Dame Judi Dench?

Would you rather...

have sex with the 4 out of 5 dentists that recommend Trident
sugarless gum

OR

the 5th dissenting dentist?
Things to consider: Do you like rebels? Rebels with tooth decay?

YOU MUST CHOOSE!

Would you rather have sex...

on the monkey bars **OR** on a seesaw?

on you parents' bed when they are out **OR** in the room adjacent to your parents' room (separated only by a thin wall) while they are home?

in a plane restroom (mile high club) **OR** in a train restroom (4 foot high club)?

in the pit with all those balls in a Chuck E. Cheese play area **OR** in a convertible while it is going through a carwash?

on a bed of nails in private **OR** on a luxuriously soft bed at Mattress Discounters during a Columbus Day sale?

YOU MUST CHOOSE!

Would you rather...

have sex with Bono **OR** Elvis in his prime?

Jason Mraz **OR** Jack Johnson?

Dave Matthews **OR** Rob Thomas?

Things to consider: What if each serenaded you first?

Would you rather...

have sex with Beyoncé **OR** Christina Aguilera?

Madonna now **OR** Britney Spears when she turns 50?

Lindsay Lohan sober **OR** Lindsay Lohan messed up?

Would you rather...

have sex with a *die-hard liberal who's conservative in bed*

OR

a *die-hard conservative who's liberal in bed?* Who'd you rather marry?

YOU MUST CHOOSE!

Would you rather...

bang the office hottie on your boss's desk

OR

your high school crush in the principal's office?

Would you rather...

have sex with Steve Carell **OR** Stephen Colbert?

Derek Jeter **OR** Kobe Bryant?

Joel McHale **OR** Robert Downey, Jr.?

Tom Colicchio **OR** Simon Cowell?

The Manning brothers **OR** the Jonas Brothers?

YOU MUST CHOOSE!

Would you rather...

have sex with Kristin Kreuk **OR** Brooke Burke?

Marisa Miller **OR** Adriana Lima?

Sharon Stone in her prime **OR** Kathy Ireland in her prime?

Minka Kelly **OR** Minka the porn star (world's largest-breasted Asian)?

Pelbin Frolkdarp **OR** Lelsgahn Nasklope? (Go with your instinct.)

YOU MUST CHOOSE!

BAD BREAKS: WEIRD, WILD, AND WARPED

For reasons beyond your understanding, you are about to be stricken with a terrible curse: a crazy compulsion, a deranged deformity, a perplexing personality disorder, or some other brutal-for-you, entertaining-for-everyone-else affliction. Sometimes, a curse can turn out to be a blessing in disguise. Other times, not so much…

Would you rather...

impulsively shout "Follow that car, and step on it!" every time
you get into a vehicle

OR

invariably start all your sentences with "Negro, please!"?

Would you rather...

have orange Jell-O phlegm

OR

have glittered sweat?
Things to consider: possible stripper career

Would you rather...

for the rest of your life, have a two inch splinter of wood inescapably
stuck in your head

OR

have the song "Afternoon Delight" inescapably stuck in your head?

YOU MUST CHOOSE!

Would you rather...

compulsively police-frisk everyone you meet until "they're clear"

OR

passionately kiss anyone and everyone whenever you say goodbye?

Would you rather...

only be able to express your feelings by bursting into Broadway-style song and dance

OR

only by using PowerPoint presentations complete with charts and graphs?

Would you rather...

realize you have gum caught in your pubic hair

OR

realize you have pubic hair caught in your gum (after five minutes of chewing)?

Things to consider: This question excerpted from the *Socratic Dialogues*.

YOU MUST CHOOSE!

Would you rather...

hear all music in 8-bit Nintendo DS sound quality

OR

mistakenly push on every "pull" door for two minutes before figuring it out?

Would you rather...

automatically bitch slap anyone you're speaking with who makes a grammatical error

OR

be able to defecate only in birdhouses?

Would you rather...

have a government agent on three-way calling for all of your phone calls

OR

have an attention-seeking Dane Cook on three-way for all your calls?

YOU MUST CHOOSE!

Would you rather...

have a harelip

OR

lip hair?

Things to consider: Lip hair is comprised of a dozen 10-inch-long hairs which cannot be cut.

Would you rather...

have all your text messages broadcast on highway amber alert signs

OR

have all your text messages sent to your parents?

Would you rather...

always have to be talking to stay awake

OR

always have to be moving at least 1 mph?

YOU MUST CHOOSE!

Would you rather...

have surgically implanted bull's horns

OR

surgically implanted bull's balls?

Things to consider: the extra weight

Would you rather...

only be able sleep sharing a bed with a manatee

OR

only be able to shower with the Wayans brothers?

Would you rather...

be stuck in a North Korean prison with Jackie Chan

OR

MacGyver?

YOU MUST CHOOSE!

Cats Vs. Dogs

Would you rather...

be overwhelmingly compelled to chase squirrels and mailmen like a dog

OR

have a tendency to casually crawl onto people's laps to take naps like a cat?

Would you rather...

every time you're in a car, have to hang your head out the window like a dog (including when you are driving)

OR

have to take dumps in a litter box?

YOU MUST CHOOSE!

Would you rather...

be mortally terrified of triangles

OR

of the number 4?

Things to consider: pizza slices, the dreaded isosceles, 4:44.

Would you rather...

only be able to communicate using movie quotes

OR

only be able to speak in Lolcat language?

Would you rather...

have all your dates chaperoned by WWE giant, The Big Show

OR

have to invite a pack of Mormon missionaries to every party you have?

YOU MUST CHOOSE!

Would you rather...

address all women as "Bee-yotch" for the rest of your life

OR

all men as "My Liege"?

Things to consider: business meetings, family dinners, being a contestant on a game show

Would you rather...

urinate out of your left nostril

OR

defecate only via a bio-prosthetic shoulder-mounted rocket launcher?

Things to consider: using urinals, sneezing, aiming for enemies

YOU MUST CHOOSE!

Would you rather...

have constantly sweaty (to the point of dripping) palms

OR

invariably emit a 10-second fart when hugged?

Would you rather...

have living bowel movements that are in the shape of fecal hamsters

OR

randomly puke up a dozen hermit crabs once a week?

Would you rather...

get a tattoo of an accurate ruler up your arm

OR

a tip percentage chart on the back of your hand?

YOU MUST CHOOSE!

Would you rather...

have all the steps in your house replaced with chutes and ladders

OR

have all your furniture made of adjustable Legos?

Would you rather...

fashion underwear out of crumb-filled potato chip bags

OR

wear socks full of centipedes?

YOU MUST CHOOSE!

Would you rather...

have broccoli hair

OR

croissant skin?

Things to consider: healthy snack hair cut, flaking

Would you rather...

lose your teeth every week like a Tiger Shark

OR

shed your skin once a week like a snake?

Would you rather...

have your skin made out of sticky Wacky Wall Walker material

OR

have your body made out of Nerf material?

Things to consider: constantly collecting dirt and lint, getting really heavy in the swimming pool

YOU MUST CHOOSE!

Would you rather...

have to "log-roll" anytime you are standing still to avoid falling over

OR

perpetually have involuntary movements as if you are swatting gnats out of your face?

Would you rather...

compulsively head-butt anything you see that's purple

OR

compulsively make out with anything orange?

Things to consider: eggplant, pumpkins, grapes, carrots, Grimace, Oompa-Loompas

YOU MUST CHOOSE!

Would you rather...

be reincarnated as Paris Hilton's toy poodle

OR

Britney Spears' next baby?

Would you rather...

have a rare Tourette's syndrome that causes you to always flip off police officers

OR

one where you uncontrollably moon nuns?

YOU MUST CHOOSE!

Would you rather...

every time you cry, one person is cured of cancer for every tear

OR

every time you get the hiccups, a random Al Qaeda member is killed for each hiccup?

Would you rather...

have a seven-foot-long tongue

OR

seven-foot-long neck?

Would you rather...

have a helium-filled body

OR

a lead-filled body?

YOU MUST CHOOSE!

Would you rather...

have your two top front teeth never stop growing

OR

your two bottom front teeth never stop growing?
Things to consider: vision problems, walking problems

Would you rather...

compulsively engage mailmen in sumo contests to try to belly them off your doorstep

OR

compulsively challenge all baristas to arm wrestle?

Would you rather...

have an actual beehive hairdo

OR

have actual mutton chop sideburns?

YOU MUST CHOOSE!

Would you rather...

have a solar-powered brain

OR

a battery-powered brain?

Things to consider: Who would have your extra battery?, slowing down as power gets low, cloudy days, where would you live?

Would you rather...

occasionally "lose reception" (like when on a cell phone) in conversation and be unable to hear what people are saying

OR

have a belly button that is a black hole that sucks objects within two inches into nothingness?

Would you rather...

snore the sound of a chainsaw

OR

burp with the force of a bathroom hair dryer?

YOU MUST CHOOSE!

Would you rather...

have to wear a Snuggie in public every day

OR

have to wear an eye patch?

Things to consider: playing sports, business presentations, sleeping on airplanes

Would you rather...

have to drink using only an eye dropper

OR

have to eat using only a thumbtack?

Would you rather...

have to keep a hard-boiled egg in your mouth at all times

OR

have an armadillo chained to your leg at all times?

YOU MUST CHOOSE!

CHAPTER TWENTY-ONE

21

POWERS

Change isn't always bad. Sometimes the best thing that can happen to you is being forced to find a new job, having to move on from an unhealthy relationship, or being beamed with high-potency gamma rays granting you the very minor power to levitate muffins. As you contemplate the following questions, remember: "With great power, comes great responsibility." And remember also: "With very limited power comes very limited responsibility."

Would you rather...

have the ability to extend yellow lights at traffic signals by 5 seconds

OR

be able to refill your gas tank by playing *Air Supply's Greatest Hits* in its entirety on your car stereo?

Would you rather...

for one day a month be able to save your life and reload like in a computer game

OR

be able to musically "montage" in three minutes vast amounts of learning and/or training that would normally take three months?

Would you rather...

have all your blackheads produce beluga caviar when squeezed

OR

have all your whiteheads turn into pearls over the course of a year?

YOU MUST CHOOSE!

Would you rather...

have psychic visions of available mall parking spots

OR

have the preternatural ability to always choose the fastest checkout line?

Would you rather...

be visited by the "Ghost of Your Sexual Experiences Past"

OR

the "Ghost of Your Sexual Experiences Future"?
Things to consider: What would each show you? What would you learn from it?

Would you rather...

be able to mentally watch any DVD by slipping it into your butt crack

OR

be able to get an Internet connection anywhere as long as you're pinching your nipples?

YOU MUST CHOOSE!

455

Would you rather...

psychically know all the phone prompts to expediently get you to
a live customer service person

OR

have the ability to see through egg cartons at the grocery store
and know if any of the eggs inside are broken?

Would you rather...

have astonishing ordering instincts and make perfect menu choices in
3.5 seconds

OR

have amazing luck at finding parking spaces with extra time left
on the meter?

Would you rather...

be able to change any lamp into Whoopi Goldberg

OR

vice-versa?
Things to consider: How would you use your powers?

YOU MUST CHOOSE!

Would you rather...

be able to see every human's "expiration date"

OR

not?

Things to consider: Dude, that's deep.

Would you rather...

have the ability to mute another person like a TV

OR

be able to change your voice to a Spanish voice-over?

Things to consider: vacationing in Madrid, nagging moms, petulant kids, petulant day-laborers

Would you rather...

have a vagina that can magically validate any parking pass

OR

that can comfortably hold all the contents of your purse?

(Men: Read as "have a partner with...")

YOU MUST CHOOSE!

Would you rather...

have a penis that comes in handy as a bottle opener

OR

a cigarette lighter?

Would you rather...

have retractable claws

OR

functional gills?
Things to consider: tree climbing, necking

YOU MUST CHOOSE!

Would you rather...

have corkscrew toenails **OR** have potato-peeling fingernails?

have silverware fingernails **OR** lockpick toenails?

a retractable toenail knife **OR** a retractable middle fingernail extender that accomplishes the effect of giving the finger?

Would you rather...

have an avatar that is an eagle-creature **OR** panther-creature?

wolf-creature **OR** spider-creature?

emu-creature **OR** Paula Poundstone-creature?

Would you rather...

have lemon-flavored hangnails

OR

have denim scabs?

YOU MUST CHOOSE!

Would you rather...

have the ability to will food to fall out of vending machines

OR

be born with a calculator on your ankle?

Would you rather...

be able to summon swarms of bugs

OR

be able to kill bugs with mini-lasers shot from your eyes?

Would you rather...

be able to spit with the force of a blow dart gun

OR

teleport the gas of your farts anywhere within a 100-foot radius?

Things to consider: killing birds, killing careers

YOU MUST CHOOSE!

Would you rather...

be able to eat unlimited food without gaining weight

OR

be able to eat free in any restaurant?

Would you rather...

have x-ray peripheral vision

OR

have the ability to hear anything exactly 147 feet away?

Would you rather...

be able to come in fourth in any race any time

OR

be able to perfectly forge anyone's handwriting but only when writing the phrase "I want pudding!"

Things to consider: selling forged President Obama-signed photos (where he evidently wants everyone to know he wants pudding).

YOU MUST CHOOSE!

Would you rather...

have eyes that can make anyone you want fall in love with you

OR

have eyes that can turn your enemies to stone?

Would you rather...

have skin that lathers whenever you get wet

OR

have refrigerated pockets?

Things to consider: swimming, reaching into your pockets on hot days

Would you rather...

have the ability to communicate with poodles **OR** pit bulls?

kittens **OR** elephants?

socks **OR** bagels?

YOU MUST CHOOSE!

Would you rather...

be given life-long "butting in line" privileges

OR

life-long "profanity at any time" privileges?

Would you rather...

have an hour-long chat with your 15-year-old self

OR

with your 60-year-old self?

Things to consider: What would you say? What would you ask?

Would you rather...

be able to cure cases of malaria by holding your hand against the foreheads of the infirmed

OR

be able to telekinetically deliver titty-twisters?

YOU MUST CHOOSE!

Would you rather...

every time you sneeze, a $20 bill is hidden somewhere in your house

OR

every time you poop, a $100 bill is hidden somewhere inside the BM?

Would you rather...

have the ability to shrink down to one inch in height

OR

the ability to grow to 100 feet in height?

Would you rather...

have a tape measurer tongue

OR

be able to blow into your own body to make it a flotation device?

YOU MUST CHOOSE!

Would you rather...

have ear speakers that broadcast whatever music you imagine in your head

OR

have the ability to make anyone speak in a Jamaican accent?

Would you rather...

have the ability to control the movements of ants

OR

be able to communicate with birds to direct them exactly where to poop?

YOU MUST CHOOSE!

Would you rather...

have a pony tail lasso

OR

have elastic testicles which you use like a mace to fight crime?

Would you rather...

have anything you touch turn to gold **OR** to Silly Putty?

silver **OR** Nerf?

cheese **OR** become helium-filled?

Things to consider: touching furniture, pets, family, friends, enemies

YOU MUST CHOOSE!

The Poo-Poo/Pee-Pee Page

Would you rather...

poop fragrant potpourri bundles

OR

be able to beam your pee from your bladder to the toilet?

Things to consider: never having to hold it, leaving bathrooms smelling great

Would you rather...

have your poop come out in a perfectly-stacked pyramid of spheres (like cannon balls)

OR

be able to poop complex domino set ups?

YOU MUST CHOOSE!

Would you rather...

be able to talk to any animal

OR

be able to change into any animal?

Would you rather...

have the ability to see the future, but only one second ahead

OR

have the ability to fly, but only in the inside of airplanes?

Would you rather...

produce fudge in your belly button

OR

be able to fart the tune of any song?

YOU MUST CHOOSE!

Would you rather...

have the ability to temporarily swap your parents with your friends' parents

OR

have the ability to temporarily swap facial features with your friends?

Would you rather...

be able to stop and rewind your life

OR

have a cheat code that allows you to jump ahead and skip parts of your life?

YOU MUST CHOOSE!

Would you rather...

be able to scan documents into your computer with your tongue

OR

be able to weed-whack your lawn with your foot?

Would you rather...

have eyes that can change color to match your outfit

OR

tan in the pattern of desert camouflage?

Would you rather...

have Lego boogers

OR

Lincoln-Log poops?

YOU MUST CHOOSE!

Would you rather...

have thunder and lightning crack every time you arch your eyebrow

OR

have the ability to magically control anyone's hair?

Would you rather...

urinate rainbow colors

OR

fart the works or Rachmaninoff?

Would you rather...

be told the answer to the 439th most interesting question in the universe by God

OR

get $50,000?

YOU MUST CHOOSE!

Would you rather...

have one solid gold toe

OR

diamond nipples?

Would you rather...

have an iPhone app that gives you the exact location of any missing pet

OR

the location of nearby people named Millard?

Would you rather...

have an entire department of the CIA devoted to providing you up-to-the-minute information on all of your exes

OR

your boss?

YOU MUST CHOOSE!

Would you rather...

be able to toast bread with your armpits

OR

blend food into smoothies by sticking your pinkie into a glass?

Would you rather...

have the ability to mentally control ferrets **OR** parrots?

bees **OR** sheep?

dice **OR** toupees?

Would you rather...

have foldable Swiss army knife devices for fingernails

OR

have nunchucks for hair?

YOU MUST CHOOSE!

Would you rather...

be the best hopscotcher in the world

OR

the best air guitarist?

Dragon Age: Origins players only:

Would you rather...

have the pure power of Shale the golem

OR

a rune of +15 damage to Darkspawn?

YOU MUST CHOOSE!

SEX CHANGE

In an era where Internet Porn is consumed like a daily vitamin, and a Cleveland Steamer is considered second base, you might think it would be harder to make your sex life odder than it already is. Guess again. Your sex life is about to get a whole lot more interesting.

Would you rather...

the strength of your erection directly correlate to the number of service bars on your cell phone

OR

have an erection which, like a compass, always points north?
Things to consider: switching to Verizon, camping in the West Virginia wilderness, "spotty coverage"; (Women: substitute "your partner's erection").

Would you rather...

never be able to use the Internet for porn again

OR

never be able to use the Internet for legitimate purposes again?
(Women: substitute "Celebrity gossip" for "porn")

Would you rather...

orgasm once every five seconds, five minutes, five years

OR

high five?
Things to consider: your job, your marriage, your pick-up basketball games

YOU MUST CHOOSE!

Would you rather...

have all your sexual experiences narrated like a nature documentary by Sir David Attenborough

OR

sarcastically commented on by the robots from *Mystery Science Theater 3000*?

Would you rather...

have nipples that have fused into each other like a fleshy handle

OR

have extra nipples in the palms of your hands?

Things to consider: ease of arousal, stumping palm-readers, shaking hands at business meetings

Would you rather...

live with a permanent erection of 1 inch

OR

19 inches?

Things to consider: sex, potential for injury, tucking into your sock

YOU MUST CHOOSE!

Would you rather your porn name be...

First name = your middle name; Last name = the first street you grew up on

OR

First name = favorite meteorological adjective (Stormy, Misty, Snowy, Dewy); Last name = favorite substance (Diamond, Stone, Wood, etc.)?

Would you rather your porn name be...

First name = state you're from; Last name = surname of the celebrity you most look like

OR

First name = any Nyquil-alleviated symptom (Stuffy, Coughing, Sneezing, Aching, etc); Last name = Last name of closest Jewish friend?

YOU MUST CHOOSE!

Would you rather...

have a maximum time limit of 3 minutes to complete all your sex acts

OR

a minimum time of 3 hours—(if you climax before then, you have to start over)?

Would you rather...

your orgasm face appear on all of your photo IDs

OR

always exhibit a perfect emotionless poker face and speak in a monotone during sex, including orgasm?

Would you rather have to seduce people using only...

origami **OR** shadow puppets?

a kazoo **OR** parkour?

planking **OR** prop comedy?

YOU MUST CHOOSE!

Right before you approach orgasm, would you rather...

have your adorable pet kitten nuzzle up against you

OR

have your grandmother leave an audible message on your answering machine?

Would you rather...

during sex, thrust to the rhythm of opening bars

of "Eye of the Tiger" **OR** "Twinkle Twinkle Little Star"?

YOU MUST CHOOSE!

Would you rather...

have a bizarre condition where your penis is 12 inches when limp
but only 3 inches when erect

OR

one that is 28 inches limp and 6 inches erect?

Things to consider: tying it around your waist like a sweatshirt; rolling it up like a snail shell

Would you rather...

make a progressively higher-pitched, whistling teakettle sound
as you approach orgasm

OR

feel the kickback force of a shotgun when climaxing?

Would you rather...

have your climax always interrupted by a phone call from your mom

OR

by Kanye West rushing in and saying, "I'ma let you finish..."
and then launching into some inappropriate speech?

YOU MUST CHOOSE!

Would you rather...

be able to have sex with any partner, once

OR

be able to have sex as many times as you want
but with only one partner?

Would you rather...

(Men) be celibate except one day per decade with your choice of
Victoria's Secret supermodel

OR

be married to a nymphomaniac Kirstie Alley?

YOU MUST CHOOSE!

Would you rather...

have your genitals located on the small of your back
OR
on your left shoulder?

Would you rather...

permanently have your genitals shifted 3 inches to the left **OR** rotated 45 degrees counter-clockwise?

4 inches to the left **OR** rotated 180 degrees?

3 inches to the left **OR** 3 inches higher up?

YOU MUST CHOOSE!

Which of the following strange venereal diseases would you endure if you had to choose one? Which would you least want?

- Alaskan King Crabs
- Eyeball herpes
- Constantly expanding testicles
- an STD that causes a burning sensation when you urinate
- an STD that makes the sound of a bagpipe when you defecate?
- an STD that makes your genitals ooze pickle juice
- an STD that makes your penis lighter than air
- an STD that makes your penis a tension-coiled spring like an April Fool's peanut brittle novelty snake
- an STD that makes you think you are Federal Reserve Chairman Ben Bernanke during sex

YOU MUST CHOOSE!

Would you rather...

have ragtime music magically play any time you have sex

OR

have '70s porn music start to play every time you say something that could be interpreted as double entendre no matter where you are?

Things to consider: "I just need to 'file this memo'."

Would you rather...

be compelled to dry-hump anyone you encounter wearing a visor

OR

have your crotch and left eye exchange places?

Things to consider: poker games, eye patches, golf courses

Would you rather...

all attractive people were severely allergic to your genitals

OR

all of your sexual partners henceforth develop Post Traumatic Stress Disorder?

YOU MUST CHOOSE!

Would you rather...

have a penis that works as a metal detector

OR

a laser pointer?

Would you rather...

never be able to watch porn again for the rest of your life

OR

only be able to watch porn for the rest of your life?

Would you rather...

have sex always take as long as it takes you to complete
the *TV Guide* crossword puzzle

OR

as long as it takes for you to complete the *New York Times* Tuesday
crossword puzzle?

YOU MUST CHOOSE!

Would you rather...

always utter the names of state capitals while climaxing **OR** Biblical quotes?

Greek gods **OR** really bad sound effects of machine guns, explosions, helicopters, etc.?

"Here comes the trolley!" **OR** the song "Flash Gordon" by Queen?

Would you rather...

have the only sexual foreplay that works for you be eyeball stimulation **OR**
having your partner fake you out by pretending to throw a tennis ball?
Things to consider: optometrist visits, challenge/pleasure of taking your contacts out, "Where'd it go? Where'd that ball go?! Yay!"

Would you rather...

have breast implants filled with M&Ms **OR** peanut M&Ms?

bacon bits **OR** living chinchillas?

an entire world like that on the flower in *Horton Hears a Who* **OR** the spirit of Leif Erikson?

YOU MUST CHOOSE!

Would you rather...

during sexual congress, be unable to get Burl Ives' "Holly Jolly Christmas" out of your head

OR

be unable to shake the image of the Harlem Globetrotters?

Would you rather...

while in the throes of passion, accidentally yell out the name of your ex **OR** yell out the name of your partner's mother?

a friend of the same sex's name **OR** your own name?

Would you rather...

only be attracted to freckled, redheaded Asians

OR

albinos under 5'2" with 1400+ SAT scores and 0-negative blood type?

YOU MUST CHOOSE!

Would you rather...

upon orgasm, ejaculate a cup of honey

OR

a gallon of gasoline?

Things to consider: tea, rising gas prices, bear attacks, your carbon footprint

Would you rather...

have an incredible-looking body that is completely sexually nonfunctional

OR

a hideous-looking body that performs amazingly sexually and experiences terrific sensation?

Would you rather...

have cowbells for nipple piercings

OR

pieces of string with helium balloons on the end?

YOU MUST CHOOSE!

Pick-a-Penis!

Women: Read as "have a partner with..."

Would you rather...

have a penis that is coated with chloroform **OR** one that requires the use of a bike tire pump to get erect?

a light-saber penis **OR** a heatable branding iron penis with your initials on the head?

a penis with a tiny rhinoceros horn on the tip **OR** a penis that wriggles like a snake whenever you hear music?

YOU MUST CHOOSE!

Vexing Vaginas!

Men: Read as "have a partner with…"

Would you rather...

have a greeting card microchip implanted in your vagina that plays "Feliz Navidad" every time you spread your legs **OR** one that makes the sound of an air horn at orgasm?

a vagina that shoots a barrage of camera flashes like the paparazzi when it gets aroused **OR** one that attracts the paparazzi when it gets aroused?

Things to consider: obstacles to oral sex, pictures on gossip sites

YOU MUST CHOOSE!

If you had to choose one of the following pubic haircuts, which would you choose?

The Don King

Flock of Seagulls

Corn Rows

Lionel Richie-style Jheri curls

1880s Circus Muscleman Handlebar Mustache

YOU MUST CHOOSE!

Would you rather...

(men) have your testicles and eyeballs exchange places

OR

your nose and penis?

Things to consider: scrotal surgery to create transparent holes, erections, perineum odor

Would you rather...

(women) have your nipples and eyes change places

OR

your vagina and nose?

Things to consider: cutting holes in shirts, moving to Middle East to wear burqas and veils

Note: These questions excerpted from Jean-Paul Sartre's *Being and Nothingness*.

YOU MUST CHOOSE!

Would you rather...

fart maple syrup

OR

nitrous oxide?

Would you rather...

have genitalia made of fine crystal which if shattered cannot
be repaired

OR

warped imperfect "Golem" genitalia made from a clay mold
that a 6-year-old attempted to accurately craft?

YOU MUST CHOOSE!

Nipples!

Would you rather...

have nipples that grow an inch a day for the rest of your life and curl up all crazy like those dudes who never cut their fingernails

OR

have perpetually lactating nipples (PLN's)?

Things to consider: babies suckling through crazy straw-like nipples, work as a barista

Would you rather...

have literal silver dollar nipples

OR

literal pencil eraser nipples?

Would you rather...

have nipples that can be shot as poisonous darts

OR

that work like "pop up" timers to help you know when roasts are done in the oven?

YOU MUST CHOOSE!

23

EMBARRASSING EPISODES

Putting the "bare ass" in embarrassing.

Comfortable in your own skin? What if that skin was tattooed with the periodic table? You're about to find out exactly how confident and open you truly are. Cringe and bear these gut-wrenching dilemmas featuring an embarrassment of riches and a richness of embarrassment.

Would you rather...

pole-dance naked on a freezing pole

OR

pole-dance in a g-string in front of your in-laws?

Things to consider: labia/scrotal adhesion to pole; father-in-law

Would you rather...

have all your sexual thoughts automatically tweeted to your parents

OR

vice-versa?

Would you rather...

your Facebook status automatically update with a tally of your lifetime masturbation total

OR

with the name of the person you last fantasized about?

YOU MUST CHOOSE!

Would you rather...

strip in front of your grandparents

OR

have them strip in front of you?

Would you rather...

have a sex tape turn up on the web of you and an old girlfriend/boyfriend

OR

a sex tape of you and your current partner?

Would you rather...

your ringtone be a recording of the dirtiest thing you've ever shouted in bed

OR

the rantings from a white power rally?

YOU MUST CHOOSE!

Would you rather...

butt-dial your girlfriend/boyfriend while you're complaining about them

OR

accidentally "sext" your mom?

Would you rather...

get caught picking your nose by a coworker

OR

rip a stinky, thunderous fart in the middle of an otherwise quiet staff meeting?

Would you rather...

during your wedding, have visible skid marks on your dress

OR

mistakenly say "Assmunch" instead of your partner's name during your vows?

YOU MUST CHOOSE!

Would you rather...

accidentally wet the bed when staying at someone else's house

OR

clog the toilet at a dinner party (complete with break-the-water-surface-BMs and flooding)?

Would you rather...

have Ken Burns make a five-part documentary on your adolescent masturbation habits to air on PBS

OR

have a complete written transcript of your sexual encounters available for download for $29.99 on npr.com?

Things to consider: Doris Kearns Goodwin weighing on your use of a "slut-sock"; slow dissolves from a still shot of your ecstatic face to a tube of KY Jelly; do people read?

YOU MUST CHOOSE!

Would you rather...

wear a tuxedo to work every day

OR

a UPS uniform?

Would you rather...

accidentally email your dirtiest email you've ever written to your whole address book

OR

have all of your private sing-to-yourself moments magically broadcast on YouTube?

Would you rather...

after a night of drinking, wake up next to your boss **OR** someone who works beneath you?

a close coworker **OR** your best platonic friend of the opposite sex?

a first cousin **OR** a llama?

YOU MUST CHOOSE!

Would you rather...

purposely step hard on the wedding dress train as a bride walks down the aisle at a wedding

OR

cough an audible "Boring" at a funeral?

Would you rather...

get caught attending a Miley Cyrus concert

OR

a Billy Ray Cyrus concert?

Would you rather...

have your Match.com profile written by your mother **OR** father?

your six-year-old nephew **OR** your grandmother?

your ex **OR** one of those spam email writers?

Things to consider: bitter comments from your ex; "It is with the utmost sincerity that I request you achieve a date with me. I have recently come into some money and need your company and bank routing number..."

YOU MUST CHOOSE!

Would you rather...

have to dance a ballet for two minutes in front of your entire office/class

OR

have to sing three pop songs in front of everybody?

Would you rather...

have your last named changed to "Scroteboat"

OR

"bin Laden?"

YOU MUST CHOOSE!

Would you rather...

find out your boyfriend/girlfriend has been blogging about your sex life

OR

that your parents have been blogging about theirs?

Would you rather...

have your sexual encounters watched and critiqued by a focus group of 18-35 year old males behind a one-way mirror

OR

by *America's Got Talent* judges?

Would you rather...

no matter what you are buying, have the cashier at the supermarket ask for a price check on extra small condoms
every time you get groceries

OR

every time you get groceries, have to use a checkout lane full of six old women, each paying by check?

YOU MUST CHOOSE!

Would you rather...

after a night of very heavy drinking, wake up next to this guy

OR

this guy?

YOU MUST CHOOSE!

Would you rather...

star in a herpes medication commercial as a patient for $50,000

OR

as the doctor for $5,000?

Would you rather...

slap your grandmother forcefully across the face

OR

watch the Internet video "Two Girls, One Cup" with her?

YOU MUST CHOOSE!

Would you rather be caught by your partner masturbating to...

pictures of your ex **OR** pictures of your partner's sibling?

an anime drawing **OR** a picture of a neighbor?

a framed photo of yourself **OR** lascivious pictures of Optimus Prime?

Would you rather...

compete in a spelling bee and win, but have a vicious erection the entire time

OR

go out in the first round to spare yourself further embarrassment?
(Women: Please substitute "erection" with "super-erect nipples.")

YOU MUST CHOOSE!

Would you rather...

the full catalog of your sexual experiences be available for rental on Netflix

OR

the full catalog of your parents' sexual experiences be available?

Would you rather...

be caught by your friends in possession of an illicit snuff film

OR

a David Archuleta CD?

Would you rather...

have your mother have to sign a consent form every time you perform intercourse

OR

have to fully solve the *New York Times* Crossword before doing so?

Things to consider: weekly Monday sex

YOU MUST CHOOSE!

Would you rather...

have your genitalia regularly printed on the backs of milk cartons nationwide

OR

your orgasm become a popular cell phone ring tone?

Would you rather...

have your Facebook status always show your latest sexual intercourse duration

OR

have to post at least one picture a month on your Facebook feed from one of your sexual encounters (does not have to show nudity)?

YOU MUST CHOOSE!

Would you rather...

have one sexual encounter a month reviewed and analyzed by sports commentators on ESPN

OR

have your sex life traded on the New York Stock Exchange and regularly reported on CNBC?

Things to consider: commentators using the chalkboard, slow-motion replays; your stockholders furious that you didn't have enough anal in the 4th quarter.

Would you rather...

have your sexual performance criticized by Simon Cowell once a year on national television

OR

by your girlfriend once a week at a family dinner?

YOU MUST CHOOSE!

Would you rather...

knowingly have sex with a trannie once

OR

unknowingly have sex with a trannie for a year?

Would you rather...

walk in on your parents having sex

OR

walk in on your grandparents having sex?

YOU MUST CHOOSE!

Which embarrassing fetish would you rather have?

most robust sexual arousal experienced by defecating in wallets **OR** by dressing up and being treated as a Chinese peasant rice-farmer?

unwavering need to be called "Leonard" to reach orgasm **OR** be unable to reach orgasm unless you grip He-Man dolls in both hands?

compulsion to dry-hump tortoises **OR** undeniable urge to have intercourse with grocery store gumball machines?

Things to consider: gumball machines are considered to be some of the most germ-infested objects in the world; shell scrapes

Would you rather...

have your sex life be a topic on *Meet the Press*

OR

Chelsea Lately?

YOU MUST CHOOSE!

Would you rather...

get a Dirty Sanchez

OR

not have to undergo any deviant sexual act, but have a new sex act named after you that involves giving an enema of melted cheese to one's partner and then having them rectally squeeze it out on party crackers which you two share while sipping a glass of fine port?

YOU MUST CHOOSE!

CHAPTER **24** TWENTY-FOUR

PREDICTION: PAIN

Life isn't always a bowl of cherries. Sometimes it's a bowl of cherry bombs that you have to light and then put into your mouth one by one until all of your teeth have been blown out. Such is the case with this lovingly brutal chapter where your imagination is sure to be stretched along with your eyelids, nipples, scrotums, and insides. At least you get to choose the lesser of two very, very painful evils.

Would you rather...

use an ice pick as a Q-tip

OR

use sandpaper as toilet paper?

Would you rather...

be twisted up like a balloon animal

OR

crushed like a beer can?

Would you rather...

bite into a popsicle with your front teeth 20 times

OR

get a paper cut on your eye?

YOU MUST CHOOSE!

Would you rather...

dip your hands in hot oil for 3 minutes

OR

have a circus strongman grab your ass cheeks and attempt to rip them in half like a phonebook for 30 seconds?

Would you rather...

be pegged nonstop for ten minutes with oranges **OR** eggs?

chimp feces **OR** cantaloupes?

Koosh balls **OR** paper footballs?

Would you rather...

have your face repeatedly paddled for five minutes by ping pong world champions

OR

have somebody do the "got your nose" trick and really rip off your nose?

YOU MUST CHOOSE!

Everybody has a pierce.

Would you rather...

get 5000 piercings wherever you want

OR

1 piercing in your heart?

Would you rather...

pierce your perineum

OR

your uvula?

Would you rather...

pierce your eyeball

OR

your pancreas?

YOU MUST CHOOSE!

Would you rather...

shit out 100 jacks

OR

a whole winter squash?

Would you rather...

have an adult circumcision

OR

cut off your left pinky?

Would you rather...

have a tadpole crawl up your nose and turn into a frog

OR

a spider lay an egg sac in your ear?

YOU MUST CHOOSE!

Would you rather...

have your thumbs smashed by a hammer

OR

have a 5-inch screw slowly screwed into your navel?

Would you rather...

for 60 seconds, kiss a poisonous jellyfish

OR

your mother?

Would you rather...

have to wear a nose ring that is connected to an earring
with a 2-inch chain

OR

have to wear a lip ring connected to a belly-button ring
with an 8-inch chain?

YOU MUST CHOOSE!

Would you rather...

be chased by a swarm of bees **OR** by one really angry German Shepherd?

40 angry pigeons **OR** 3 angry weathermen?

10,000 evil crickets **OR** one randy Burger King mascot?

Would you rather...

use a poison ivy condom

OR

have a sushi chef pack your urethra with fresh wasabi?

YOU MUST CHOOSE!

Would you rather...

get your finger run over by an ice skater

OR

get your balls run over by a roller-blader?

Would you rather...

be strapped to a table and have a drop of water repeatedly drip on your forehead

OR

be strapped to a table and have your eyes continuously pried open as you watch a one-week marathon of *Dora the Explorer*?

Would you rather...

have a pebble sewn into the bottom of your left foot

OR

have a sesame seed lodged uncomfortably and permanently between your front teeth?

YOU MUST CHOOSE!

Would you rather...

have to eat 25 jalapeño peppers for breakfast

OR

swallow 25 live mosquitoes?

Would you rather...

live with the certainty that at some point in your life you are going to be attacked by lions but not know when

OR

know exactly when it is going to happen?

Would you rather...

pierce a metal rod through your genitals

OR

through your nose (you can't remove it)?

YOU MUST CHOOSE!

Would you rather...

for twenty seconds, dry-hump a giant cheese grater naked

OR

stick your face in a fan with the safety plate off?

Would you rather...

get a horrible sunburn on the inside of your skin

OR

eat a salad of poison ivy?

Things to consider: Chew well so it is digested by the time it hits your digestive tract, inability to use aloe, ass-rash

YOU MUST CHOOSE!

Would you rather...

jump through a sprinkler of sulfuric acid

OR

have to keep a 200 degree gobstopper in your mouth
for 2 minutes?

Would you rather...

be used as a human piñata until something comes out of you

OR

be used as a human puck on a giant air hockey table?

Would you rather...

get body-slammed in the ring by World Wrestling Entertainment star
John Cena

OR

have to dress for a week in the pro wrestler T-shirt, underwear,
kneepads look?

YOU MUST CHOOSE!

Would you rather...

get spear-tackled by Shaq

OR

sit in a room with just him listening to the new rap album
he's been working on?

Would you rather...

be groped by a Edward Scissorhands

OR

make out with Johnny Staplermouth?

YOU MUST CHOOSE!

Would you rather...

for 20 seconds, rest the side of your face on a hot grill

OR

chisel off your thumbnail?

Would you rather...

stick your hand in a fan

OR

your finger in Tom Bergeron?

Would you rather...

pass a marble through your urethra

OR

a Wiffle ball through your ass?

YOU MUST CHOOSE!

Would you rather...

your doctor tell you that you have swine flu **OR** shingles?

Athlete's Crotch **OR** incurable anal leakage?

that your hands are turning into lobster claws **OR** you will gain 10 pounds a year for the rest of your life?

in order to survive, you can only eat hay for the rest of your life **OR** that you have "Eskimo-itis" – the condition in which you slowly but quite irreversibly turn into an Eskimo?

YOU MUST CHOOSE!

Would you rather...

have the septum of your nose torn with a staple remover

OR

your toenails shimmied off with a pocket knife?

Would you rather...

stick 400 thumbtacks in your body wherever you want

OR

stick 25 thumbtacks in your sack and use it for a pin cushion?

Would you rather...

have a lobster snap its claw onto your right nipple

OR

onto your Adam's Apple?

YOU MUST CHOOSE!

Would you... give your left nut for all the tea in China?

Would you rather...
get bombed to death by planes dropping slabs of beef
OR
drown to death in a pit of chocolate Magic Shell?

Would you rather...
get sacked by WWE's the Big Show
OR
"sacked" by WWE's the Big Show?

YOU MUST CHOOSE!

Would you rather...

have an inch-long splinter stuck in your tongue

OR

between your toes?

Would you rather...

get in a snowball fight against a major league pitcher

OR

be a tackling dummy for an NFL linebacker?

Would you rather...

French kiss dry ice

OR

your aunt?

YOU MUST CHOOSE!

Would you rather...

have your foot run over by a lawnmower

OR

cut off your lower lip with children's scissors?

Would you rather...

get a clumsy haircut using a weed-whacker

OR

shave with an electric knife?

Would you rather...

get hit by a car and become roadkill

OR

be attacked by a pack of zombie roadkill?

YOU MUST CHOOSE!

Would you rather...

suffer 1,000 mosquito bites **OR** 1,000 paper cuts?

1,000 loogies **OR** 1,000 Dutch Oven farts?

1,000 minutes of didactic Dr. Phil therapy **OR** 1,000 minutes in a closet with Michael Moore?

Would you rather...

have all of your hairs pulled out one by one

OR

all of your teeth pulled out one by one?

YOU MUST CHOOSE!

Would you rather...

use a Japanese Steak House table as a tanning bed for two minutes

OR

get "spray-tanned" by a flamethrower for 30 seconds?

Would you rather...

bungee-jump with the cord tied around your tongue

OR

around your genitals?

YOU MUST CHOOSE!

CHAPTER TWENTY-FIVE 25

LIVE IN A WORLD WHERE...

The world don't move to the beat of just one drum,
What might be right for you might not be right for some.
— Henry David Thoreau

Time to play Deity. The laws of the nation, of nature, of convention will soon bend at your whimsical will. Of course, the great Godthings of the Universe are not completely ceding their Rule. They are handing you two choices with which you may shape the planet. The final decision, however, is in your hands, which, by the way, you are presently fiendishly rubbing together, drunk with power.

Would you rather live in a world where...

wearing skinny jeans actually made you skinny while you wore them

OR

where skinny jeans were legally banned?

Would you rather live in a world where...

everyone's sexual performance was rated with reviews on Yelp.com **OR** where you are legally required to have sex with someone if they have collected at least 5,000 signatures through an online petition?

YOU MUST CHOOSE!

Would you rather live in a world where...

toilets quantify and loudly broadcast the volume/stink of your poops

OR

where ATM's announce your weight and account balance?

Would you rather live in a world where...

Sarah Palin is President

OR

Snooki from *Jersey Shore* is Secretary of State?

YOU MUST CHOOSE!

Would you rather live in a world where...

Mike Tyson is Speaker of the House

OR

where the *Real Housewives of Orange County* comprise the Supreme Court?

Would you rather live in a world where...

you could get drive-through intercom therapy with your fast food order

OR

where it was customary to get "happy endings" to every haircut?

YOU MUST CHOOSE!

Would you rather live in a world where...

men were expected to be waifish while women were allowed to let themselves go

OR

where men gave birth?

Would you rather live in a world where...

food can be downloaded

OR

where your dreams can?

YOU MUST CHOOSE!

Would you rather live in a world where...

the average penis length is 2 inches

OR

20 inches?

Would you rather live in a world where...

our laws were voted on not by Congress but instead by a public text message voting system á la *American Idol* (kids are allowed to vote) **OR** where amendments were made by posting laws online and opening a forum to everyone?

YOU MUST CHOOSE!

Would you rather live in a world where...

birds pooped hot fudge

OR

where dogs pooped rainbow sherbet?

Would you rather live in a world where...

social stature is derived from mathematical aptitude

OR

from the height of one's hair?

YOU MUST CHOOSE!

Would you rather live in a world where...

reality shows are accurately named, such as "Washed-Up-Celebrity Apprentice" and "Dancing with People Who Have Just Enough Notoriety to Still be Recognized from Their 15 Minutes of Fame"

OR

where women constantly quote chick flicks instead of guys quoting *Fletch* and *Caddyshack*?

Would you rather live in a world where...

teenagers still went to malt shops and sock-hops

OR

where senior citizens do all their shopping at Hot Topic?

YOU MUST CHOOSE!

Would you rather live in a world where...

cities are infested with floating air sharks

OR

where they are full of giant street squids?

Would you rather live in a world where...

the proportion of non-marshmallow-to-marshmallow pieces in cereal was inverted

OR

where pressing the button multiple times expedited the elevator's arrival?

YOU MUST CHOOSE!

Would you rather live in a world where...

when you orgasm, you see God

OR

when you orgasm, a delicious ham sandwich appears next to you?

Would you rather live in a world where...

everyone is required to travel via camel

OR

everyone is required to travel via presidential motorcade?

Things to consider: grocery shopping, right of way at a four-way stop sign

YOU MUST CHOOSE!

Would you rather live in a world where...

all business is conducted in Klingon

OR

where nakedness (with penis-gourd casing) was the preferred attire for formal occasions?

Would you rather live in a world...

with cherry-flavored snow

OR

with Old Spice-scented rain?

YOU MUST CHOOSE!

Would you rather live in a world without...

celebrities **OR** corporate welfare?

hurricanes **OR** monogamy?

Sarah Palin **OR** Spencer Pratt?

Would you rather live in a world where...

cell phone use causes baldness

OR

watching game shows is a laxative?

YOU MUST CHOOSE!

Would you rather live in a world where...

general trivia aptitude is a more desirable trait than athleticism

OR

where politicians must disclose their true motivations?

Would you rather live in a world where...

no one except you has a sense of humor

OR

no one except you has a sense of smell?

YOU MUST CHOOSE!

Would you rather live in a world where...

instead of shaking hands, people greet each other with purple nurples

OR

instead of making out, couples rubbed armpits together?
Things to consider: job interviews, the endings of romantic movies

Would you rather live in a world where...

regardless of where you went to sleep, every morning you always wake up naked and spooning a complete stranger

OR

once a month a siren randomly goes off and you are required to give a "rusty trombone" to the person standing nearest to you?

YOU MUST CHOOSE!

Would you rather live in a world where...

men and women had electrical plugs and sockets as genitalia

OR

where people had their genitals located on their palms?

Things to consider: needing an adapter for sex overseas, clapping or shaking hands

Would you rather live in a world where...

where fingernails were made of taffy

OR

where pubic hair was made of cotton candy?

YOU MUST CHOOSE!

Would you rather live in a world where...

it was typical to have full bars in your office like it was in the '50s

OR

where sexual harassment was permitted like it was in the '50s?

YOU MUST CHOOSE!

Would you rather...

support a law legalizing marijuana **OR** prostitution?

legalizing littering **OR** speeding?

legalizing public nudity **OR** groping Foot Locker employees?

Would you rather...

support a law lowering the drinking age to 18 **OR** the age of consent to 16?

raising the drinking age to 35 **OR** the age of consent to 25?

raising the legal smoking age to 21 **OR** capping smoking at age 40?

YOU MUST CHOOSE!

Would you rather live in...

Narnia **OR** Middle Earth?

The Matrix **OR** *Tron?*

Would you rather live in...

the normal world **OR** Oz (as in the *Wizard of...* by day, the HBO show prison by night)?

the daydreams of a 6-year-old **OR** of a 40-year-old?

YOU MUST CHOOSE!

Would you rather live in a world where...

everyone was a vegetarian

OR

everyone was bisexual?

Would you rather live in a world where...

humans had to migrate south in the winter like birds

OR

where humans gave birth to 300 babies at once, like fish, with one or two surviving past the first year?

YOU MUST CHOOSE!

Would you rather live in a world where...

everyone is allowed a maximum of six minutes of Internet access per day

OR

not?

Would you rather live in a world where...

citizens are allowed to try to beat away parking enforcement officers with Wiffle ball bats

OR

where they are allowed to loot the following stores: Just Lamps, Jo-Ann Fabrics, and Big and Tall shops?

YOU MUST CHOOSE!

Would you rather live in a world where...

every day was in the tone of a teen melodrama **OR** a suspense thriller?

a romantic comedy **OR** a porn?

Real World/Road Rules challenge **OR** a horror movie?

Would you rather live in a world where...

bugs are the only viable food source

OR

where the only piece of entertainment was parades?

YOU MUST CHOOSE!

Would you rather live in a world where...

Gilbert Gottfried has a complete monopoly on all voiceover work

OR

Heidi Montag delivers all nightly news based on what she is concerned with?

Would you rather live in a world where...

fog has the stench of a nauseating fart cloud

OR

where wind insults you with increasing pace and cruelness as it picks up?

YOU MUST CHOOSE!

Would you rather live in a world where...

houses are made of gingerbread and candy

OR

where motorized Big Wheels are the primary mode of transportation?

Would you rather live in a world where...

humans were the size of ants

OR

where rabbis were the size of oak trees?

YOU MUST CHOOSE!

Would you rather live in...

the mind of Jessica Simpson

OR

Charles Manson?

Would you rather live in a world where...

cops had the speed of the Flash

OR

where homeless people had the power of flight?

YOU MUST CHOOSE!

WORK AND OFFICE

More than half our life is spent on the job. As species, only the ant and the beaver spend more time working. In fact, the duck-billed platypus spends only two minutes a day working (hunting for food) while spending the rest of the day dry-humping coral (look it up). While we can't all make a living dry-humping coral (or can we?), we can imagine ways to liven up our workplace. Cast a vote on the office politics below.

Would you rather...

commute to work on a jetpack

OR

in a rickshaw?

Would you rather...

work in an office with a nap room

OR

a room where you can break objects against the wall when you're angry?

Would you rather...

have the average work day be in the tone of a screwball comedy

OR

in the tone of a kung fu movie?

Things to consider: copier highjinks, water cooler escapades, using a mouse like nunchucks, learning how to spell nunchucks

YOU MUST CHOOSE!

Would you rather...

your office or cubicle had a magnetic force that kept out anyone you didn't like

OR

a portal that went straight to any one place you desired?

Would you rather...

have a magic business card where whatever you write on it becomes your job for a day

OR

never have to work again?

Note: Sell dumb idea to Hollywood.

YOU MUST CHOOSE!

Would you rather...

be a professional pooper scooper **OR** a prison guard?

a video chat sex actor **OR** a rodeo clown?

George Bush's proofreader **OR** John Madden's masseuse?

Would you rather...

possess a special Jedi mind trick where you can avoid doing things at work that you don't want to do

OR

be able to print any image you think of in your mind?

Things to consider: "I am not the account director you are looking for."

YOU MUST CHOOSE!

These are the circumstances. You and your fellow office workers are pitted against each other in a fight to the death. Each gladiator is allowed one office supply to use as a weapon.

Would you rather fight with...

a stapler **OR** a staple remover?

binder clips **OR** rubber bands?

a hole-puncher **OR** label maker?

one of those compressed-air cans you use to clean keyboards **OR** a mug of coffee?

the copier **OR** paper clips?

Things to consider: describe your technique.

YOU MUST CHOOSE!

Would you rather...

work in cubicles stacked vertically like a Japanese driving range

OR

where each cubicle contains a private toilet and stall door?

Would you rather...

work in an office with no chairs **OR** no windows?

no talking **OR** no Internet?

no lunch **OR** no Fatheads of NBA great Ralph Sampson?

YOU MUST CHOOSE!

Would you rather...

have sex with your choice of coworker with no repercussions

OR

punch your choice of coworker with no repercussions?

Would you rather...

have your office chair replaced with a unicycle

OR

a steel pole with a two-inch diameter?

Would you rather...

have the stall doors removed in the bathroom

OR

have to wipe with Post-it notes?

YOU MUST CHOOSE!

Would you rather...

have your morning commute always be a high-speed race with cops
(if you make it to your office parking lot, you don't get a ticket)

OR

have paintball wars every lunch (winner does not have to work
in the afternoon)?

Would you rather...

have your own commuter lane on the highway

OR

have the car of your choice but no commuter lane?

YOU MUST CHOOSE!

Would you rather...

be fired for freezing your company's computer network
by surfing for too much porn

OR

for getting drunk at the office holiday party and loudly propositioning
your boss?

Would you rather...

outsource all the annoying parts of your job

OR

outsource all the responsibilities of your personal life?

YOU MUST CHOOSE!

Would you rather...

to fulfill a fantasy, receive oral sex while driving

OR

while sitting at your office desk?

Would you rather...

have sex with all the members of your office's IT department

OR

the janitorial staff?

YOU MUST CHOOSE!

Would you rather...

become internationally famous for your booger art

OR

for being an obnoxious reality show star?

Would you rather...

be a gardener with severe allergies **OR** a high school math teacher with problem flatulence?

a blind matador **OR** a quadraplegic luger?

a dyslexic eye doctor **OR** a deaf/mute ventriloquist?

YOU MUST CHOOSE!

Would you rather...

give all business presentations in mime

OR

in the persona and attire of ex-WWE wrestler the Mountie?

Would you rather...

have a calendar in your office of the 12 largest human poops of the past year

OR

the 12 most embarrassing pictures ever taken of you?

Idea for book: *Stinkblots*—like inkblots, but featuring pictures of different fecal creations from which you describe what you images emerge: a butterfly, a caterpillar, your mother, etc.

YOU MUST CHOOSE!

Would you rather...

your boss looked like Megan Fox/George Clooney but acts like a boot camp drill seargant

OR

looked like the Elephant Man but is supportive and encouraging?

Would you rather...

commute to work daily in a Lexus in horrible rush hour traffic

OR

have a quick painless commute but have to drive in a van with a massive Wizard fantasy scene airbrushed on the side?

YOU MUST CHOOSE!

Would you rather...

only be able to communicate with coworkers via email **OR** walkie-talkie?

lifeguard flags **OR** Pictionary?

carrier pigeon **OR** a language consisting of slaps and caresses to the face?

Would you rather...

work at a company where promotions were awarded based on "dance-offs"

OR

battle rapping?

YOU MUST CHOOSE!

Would you rather...

work at a company where mandatory business attire consisted of covering yourself solely in Post-it notes

OR

wearing a sombrero, an "Oh, Snap!" half-shirt, a thong, and snowshoes?

Would you rather...

work where they offer a free 4-star-restaurant lunch every day

OR

guilt-free "happy ending" massages every day?

Would you rather...

Oscar Gamble be your boss

OR

your lover?

YOU MUST CHOOSE!

Would you rather...

have to work an 18-hour work day every day

OR

have a 3-hour work day but have to make out with the rest of the employees for 45 minutes each day?

Would you rather...

work as the assistant to (insert least favorite celebrity)

OR

as the personal wiper of (insert favorite celebrity)?

YOU MUST CHOOSE!

Would you rather...

work in Big Tobacco **OR** Big Oil?

Big Pharma **OR** Big Coal?

Big Sock **OR** Big Muffin?

Would you rather...

get paid in pennies

OR

get paid your accrued salary once every three years?

YOU MUST CHOOSE!

27

WHO'D YOU RATHER...?
(NON-SEXUAL)

It has been said that the best way to judge a person is by the company he keeps. Batman is no better than Robin. The Scarecrow's worth? Dictated by Mrs. King. Hardcastle: McCormick. Simon? Simon. So choose your friends wisely. And choose your enemies wisely-er.

Would you rather have to solve crimes teamed up with...

Gary Busey **OR** Jessica Simpson?

Betty White **OR** Donald Trump?

your mother **OR** your father?

Would you rather...

be tennis partners with Kim Jong-il

OR

a drunken Mel Gibson?

Things to consider: angry rants

YOU MUST CHOOSE!

Would you rather...

battle to the death 30 parakeets

OR

5 possessed watermelons?

Would you rather...

have to mitigate a cock-block by President Obama

OR

Brad Pitt?

Would you rather...

find out your real father is a serial rapist in jail

OR

Glenn Beck?

YOU MUST CHOOSE!

Would you rather...

have a minstrel

OR

a butler?

Would you rather...

go on a mythical quest with a wizard fresh out of rehab

OR

an anti-Semitic elf ranger?

YOU MUST CHOOSE!

Would you rather...

be raised by wolves

OR

by Paula Abdul?

Would you rather...

have the ghost of Freud as your therapist

OR

have the ghost of George Washington Carver as your personal chef?

Things to consider: winning the science fair, peanut pie, peanut butter-covered peanuts, peanut smoothies, peanut forks

YOU MUST CHOOSE!

Would you rather...

French-kiss Liza Minnelli **OR** a bowl of sliced jalapeño peppers?

your aunt **OR** a pile of fish hooks?

the inside of a bowling shoe and ball **OR** (insert the ugliest or most disgusting person you know)?

Would you rather...

that your house was designed by Dr. Seuss

OR

M.C. Escher?

YOU MUST CHOOSE!

Would you rather...

your dreams were written by Judd Apatow

OR

James Cameron?

Would you rather...

have a political roundtable interview/discussion with Joe Biden, Sinbad, and Stone Cold Steve Austin

OR

Scott Baio, former Pakistani president President Pervez Musharraf, and Kendra Wilkinson?

YOU MUST CHOOSE!

Would you rather be Facebook friends with...

Spock **OR** Yoda?

an insanely rapidly status-updating Flash **OR** an Apache Chief who brags often about the tail he gets?

Wolverine **OR** Optimus Prime?

Things to consider: "Feeling good after eating a muffin, I am"; "Today I am feeling N/A?"

Would you rather...

share a bottle of whiskey with Vladimir Putin

OR

Robin Williams?

YOU MUST CHOOSE!

Would you rather...

follow the channeled Twitter of the ghost of Socrates

OR

Groucho Marx?

Would you rather battle in the water...

3 manatees **OR** 300 flounder?

20,000 guppies **OR** 1 swordfish?

5 beavers **OR** Aquaman while he is busy doing his taxes?

YOU MUST CHOOSE!

As you try to court a lady, who would you rather have hiding in the bushes feeding you lines like Cyrano de Bergerac...

Shakespeare **OR** Snoop Dogg?

Dennis Miller **OR** Charles Barkley?

Rocco Siffredi **OR** the Snausages mascot?

YOU MUST CHOOSE!

If you could travel through time, would you rather...

"pants" Benito Mussolini during a speech

OR

moon Joseph Stalin?

If you could travel through time, would you rather...

play Truth or Dare with all of the U.S. presidents

OR

play dodgeball against an array of conquistadors?

Things to consider: Who's the ugliest chick Chester A. Arthur nailed?; beaming Hernando Cortez in the nuts

YOU MUST CHOOSE!

If you could travel through time, would you rather...

play beer pong with the founding fathers

OR

go surfing with the ancient Greek philosophers?

Would you rather...

go to a strip bar with the nine Supreme Court justices

OR

go to a Supreme Court trial with nine strippers?

YOU MUST CHOOSE!

Which one of these people would you most want to slip some LSD?

Senator John McCain before a debate?

NBC News host Brian Williams before a broadcast?

your math teacher before class?

your boss before a presentation?

an endangered white rhinoceros?

Would you rather...

be followed everywhere by a police detective watching your every step

OR

a panhandling mummy?

YOU MUST CHOOSE!

For a night on the town, who would you rather have as your wingman?

the AFLAC duck?

Chad Ochocinco?

Pat Sajak?

Optimus Prime?

Triumph the Insult Comic Dog?

Ghostface Killah from the Wu-Tang Clan?

YOU MUST CHOOSE!

Would you rather have an entourage of...

giggling, prepubescent teens **OR** corrupt Turkish politicians?

stoned surfers **OR** forlorn rodeo clowns?

a pack of raccoons **OR** day laborers?

Would you rather...

spend a year in a space station with Britney Spears in a crazy phase **OR**
a sleazy, always-hitting-on-you Count Chocula?

YOU MUST CHOOSE!

Would you rather...

share a spliff with the Dalai Lama **OR** Einstein?

Gandhi **OR** Gandalf?

your next door neighbors **OR** your teachers?

Would you rather...

fight to the death a grizzly bear **OR** 3 vampire IRS workers?

20 hostile soccer moms **OR** 6 hostile NASCAR dads?

a ninja who is looking for his keys **OR** a severely motion-sick mixed martial artist?

YOU MUST CHOOSE!

Would you rather...

fight 10 two-year-olds **OR** two 10-year-olds?

a 70-year-old **OR** 70 one-year-olds?

a 300-pound 12-year-old **OR** a 120-pound 30-year-old?

Who would you rather have as your prison cellmate?

Paris Hilton **OR** Martha Stewart?

Rush Limbaugh **OR** Carrot Top?

a really bad aspiring rap artist **OR** a dick-ish deaf dude?

YOU MUST CHOOSE!

Would you rather have to carpool to school every morning with...

Michael Moore **OR** three of the *Real Housewives of New Jersey*?

Genghis Khan **OR** Khan from *Star Trek*?

(insert most annoying person you know) **OR** (insert grossest person you know)?

Who would you rather have on your Pictionary team?

Picasso **OR** the UPS commercial guy?

YOU MUST CHOOSE!

Would you rather DJ a morning talk radio show with...

Joan Rivers **OR** Alan Greenspan?

Ricky Gervais **OR** Adam Carolla?

a lowbrow Paul Bunyan **OR** a strangely arch-conservative Johnny Appleseed?

Would you rather...

fight a creature with the body of a jaguar and the head of a cow
OR
fight a creature with the body of a horse and the head of Phil Mickelson?

YOU MUST CHOOSE!

Would you rather...

only be able to date psychiatric inmates **OR** reality show contestants?

Appalachian snake charmers **OR** Harlem Globetrotters?

close-up magicians **OR** secret agents?

Would you rather...

receive a lap dance from your sister

OR

your mother?

YOU MUST CHOOSE!

Would you rather...

share a camping tent with a PMS-ing Nancy Pelosi

OR

an extremely flirtatious otter?

Would you rather...

be high school chemistry lab partners with Bill Nye the Science Guy

OR

have Boba Fett on your school's volleyball team?

YOU MUST CHOOSE!

Would you rather...

have to share an office with Sharon Osbourne

OR

have to share toothbrushes with Gene Shalit?

You are a cannibal. Would you rather...

eat a lightly sautéed Megan Fox with braised vegetables and a white wine sauce

OR

a spicy Texas-barbecued Rachel McAdams?

YOU MUST CHOOSE!

Would you rather have your karaoke partner be...

Jason Mraz **OR** Jack Johnson?

George W. Bush's daughters **OR** his parents?

Iranian president Mahmoud Ahmadinejad **OR** Chewbacca?

YOU MUST CHOOSE!

Would you rather have a rare schizophrenia where you become convinced you are...

The Mentalist **OR** Mario from Super Mario Bros?

the world's sexiest accountant **OR** a rhythm gymnastic gold medalist mid-routine?

a glass of orange juice afraid it will spill itself **OR** the lint in the lint filter of a dryer?

YOU MUST CHOOSE!

Would you rather...

be haunted by the ghost of Ike Turner

OR

constantly get drunk-dialed by Federal Reserve Chairman Ben Bernanke?

Would you rather...

have to ride around on a lazy burro

OR

a sweaty Al Sharpton?

Would you rather...

battle 50 penguins

OR

500 sentient wallets?

YOU MUST CHOOSE!

28

WOULD YOU RATHER...?
for WOMEN

Just because you are the fairer sex, doesn't mean you can't answer foul questions. Enjoy these questions that are strong enough for a man, but PH-balanced for a woman.[1]

---

[1] Is that still a thing?

Would you rather...

be able to inflate your breasts

OR

deflate your stomach?

Would you rather...

have sex with any ex of Lindsay Lohan's

OR

Paris Hilton's?

Would you rather...

never have to take the Pill again

OR

never menstruate again?

YOU MUST CHOOSE!

Would you rather...

have sex for five straight hours but only once a month

OR

every day but only for 30 seconds?

Would you rather...

give up lube

OR

vibrators?

Would you rather...

your orgasms sound like screeching cats

OR

your voice, but through Auto Tune?

YOU MUST CHOOSE!

Would you rather hook up with...

Gerard Butler **OR** Sam Worthington?

Colin Firth **OR** Hugh Grant?

Tiger Woods **OR** T-Pain?

Would you rather...

have a three-way with your boyfriend and best friend
OR
two strangers you found on Craigslist?

YOU MUST CHOOSE!

Would you rather...

gush tears when you're aroused

OR

have your hair stand on end?

Would you rather have:

one night with Johnny Depp?

orgasms on command for the next six months?

$1 million?

YOU MUST CHOOSE!

Would you rather...

have heels that can lower into flats

OR

a weightless purse?

Would you rather...

be able to will anything to fit exactly as you want it to

OR

be able to change the dressing-room light from gross neon to a flattering glow?

Would you rather...

get a shopping spree of $1,000 at Marc Jacobs

OR

$10,000 at Target?

YOU MUST CHOOSE!

Would you rather...

be able to predict fashion trends a season in advance

OR

magically update your wardrobe to reflect current styles every year?

Would you rather...

have to sew your own clothes

OR

cut your own hair?

YOU MUST CHOOSE!

Whose style would you rather have?

Chloe Sevigny **OR** Katie Holmes?

Victoria Beckham **OR** Anna Wintour?

Kim Kardashian **OR** Snooki?

Would you rather...

make men spend a day in 4-inch heels
OR
thongs?

YOU MUST CHOOSE!

Would you rather...

have a closet the size of your bedroom, filled with designer items

OR

never have to diet again?

Would you rather...

have armpit hair that grows at 100 times the normal rate

OR

toenails that do the same thing?

Would you rather...

wax your entire body

OR

shave your head?

YOU MUST CHOOSE!

Would you rather...

have a personal masseuse

OR

personal shopper/stylist?

Would you rather...

wake up with coiffed hair

OR

minty breath?

Would you rather...

be able to get ready in five minutes

OR

have hair impervious to wind, rain and humidity?

YOU MUST CHOOSE!

Would you rather...

have legs that never needed shaving

OR

feet that pedicure themselves?

Would you rather...

be able to shrink zits with mind control

OR

have a fairy with tiny tweezers to pluck your eyebrows?

YOU MUST CHOOSE!

Would you rather...

legally change your name to Veronica Vulvatron

OR

Mons Pubis McGee?

Would you rather...

be able to shrink your exes' penises

OR

make their girlfriends uglier?

YOU MUST CHOOSE!

Would you rather...

have the ability to make your boss lose an erection

OR

get an erection?

Would you rather...

find the world's most perfect man, only to discover he has a mistress on the side

OR

that he has copious back hair and back acne?

Would you rather...

have a private jet and pilot at your disposal

OR

a brawny, dopey assistant whose only job is to pleasure you?

YOU MUST CHOOSE!

Would you rather...

have breasts that hang down to your waist

OR

have an ass that hangs down to your knees?

Would you rather...

be able to have consequence-free sex in any public place

OR

have condoms that actually do not affect sensation?

YOU MUST CHOOSE!

Would you rather...

get twelve weeks vacation per year

OR

only work three days a week?

Would you rather...

out-earn your partner

OR

make less but receive lots of extravagant gifts?

Would you rather...

time travel to live as a Suffragette

OR

flapper?

YOU MUST CHOOSE!

Would you rather...

go on a blind date with a gorgeous but dumb guy

OR

an ugly guy with a perfect penis?

Would you rather...

act in porn

OR

allow your normal sex life to be streamed on YouTube?

Would you rather...

have a home out of an interior design magazine

OR

a wardrobe out of *Vogue*?

YOU MUST CHOOSE!

Would you rather...

only need two hours of sleep per night

OR

500 calories per day?

Would you rather...

achieve world peace

OR

have perfect hair?

YOU MUST CHOOSE!

Would you rather...

never physically age past 30

OR

never emotionally age past 15?

Would you rather...

pose naked for an art class

OR

go to the beach in a thong for a whole day?

Would you rather...

blink 100 times per minute

OR

queef every 40 seconds?

YOU MUST CHOOSE!

CHAPTER TWENTY-NINE

29

WOULD YOU RATHER...?
for MEN

Gadgets! Babes! Beer! Porn! Bathroom Humor! Megan Fox! BBQ! Tits! Movies! Ass! Analysis of Neo-Marxist Dialectical Materialsim! Red Meat! Classic Movie Quotes! More Tits! Not Much Reading! iPad! Cyborgs! Lions! Tigers! Bears (not the hairy, burly, gay type!) Taffy! Sex! Slutty Celeb Pics! Uh... Rookie Cards!... hmm... running out of gas here... Bagels?... No... Did we say "Tits" yet?

Would you rather...
set off a mousetrap with your penis
OR
a bear trap with your leg?

Would you rather...
block a punt with your nuts
OR
your face?

YOU MUST CHOOSE!

Would you... have sex with Carrie Fisher now to be able to relive time and have sex with Carrie Fisher when you were 15 and she was in *Return of the Jedi?*

Would you... have sex with Kendra Wilkinson if you have to spend two weeks hanging out with her all day long first? What if you could have sex first and then had to spend two weeks hanging out afterwards (with no more sex)?

YOU MUST CHOOSE!

Would you rather...

have an app that indicates the ovulation and STD status
of potential one-night stands

OR

the number of times she's been dumped for "being crazy?"

Would you rather...

motorboat Scarlett Johansson's boobs

OR

Shakira's butt?

Would you rather...

have sex with Taylor Swift, swiftly

OR

Jenna Haze, hazily?

YOU MUST CHOOSE!

Who would make the best lesbian porn?

Cylons number six and nine from *Battlestar Galactica*?

Ginger and Mary Ann from *Gilligan's Island*?

Pocahontas and the chick from Disney's *Aladdin*?

the *Gossip Girl* cast **OR** the *True Blood* cast?

Playmate centerfolds of 1976 **OR** female *X-Men* characters?

YOU MUST CHOOSE!

Would you rather...

every time you get an erection, you get a nosebleed and vice-versa

OR

lose all sexual inhibition in the presence of nutmeg?

Would you rather...

have an erection for 3 months straight

OR

your wife/girlfriend be on her period for 3 months straight?

YOU MUST CHOOSE!

Would you rather have sex with....

Elizabeth Banks **OR** Rachel McAdams?

Naomi Watts **OR** Anna Faris?

Emmanuelle Chriqui if she was wearing Rec Specs **OR** Keeley Hazell if she was wearing gag glasses with a moustache?

Denise Milani if she were completely flat-chested and had a dumpy ass **OR** Angela Lansbury if she were a 36DD-22-34?

YOU MUST CHOOSE!

Would you rather...

see your girlfriend in a sex video on the web

OR

see your mom in a *Girls Gone Wild* tape?

Would you rather...

stick you penis in a wasp's nest

OR

in (insert disgusting acquaintance)'s mouth?

Would you rather...

that all women in the world were required to return phone calls,
no matter what

OR

that all women in the world had vaginas that recorded high scores like
video games, so you enter your initials afterward and try
to break your records?

YOU MUST CHOOSE!

Would you rather...

be caught by your mom masturbating

OR

catch your mom masturbating?
Dad?
Aunt?
Grandfather?
Dog?
Chris Hansen?

Would you rather...

watch *Twilight* 20 times in a row with your wife/girlfriend

OR

eat 5 sticks of butter?

YOU MUST CHOOSE!

Would you rather...

split a 12-pack with Jimmy Kimmel

OR

Donald Rumsfeld?

Would you rather...

play 18 holes with Tiger Woods

OR

DP 18 holes with Tiger Woods and his mistresses?

Things to consider: playing in the rough, ball-washers, other obvious golf jokes

YOU MUST CHOOSE!

Which porno would you most want to watch, imagining what the plot would be?

The Fast and Bicurious

Womb Raider

Schindler's Fist

The Incredible Bulge – (penis turns green and rips through clothes when excited)

Semento (told backwards from ejaculation all the way to putting clothes back on)

The Firm

YOU MUST CHOOSE!

Scrotum!

Would you rather...

have a zip-up change purse scrotum

OR

have a scrotum that blows up and expands into a beanbag chair?

Would you rather...

have an elastic scrotum that you can use as a nunchuck-like weapon to fight crime

OR

one made of that stress ball material that you can squeeze to reduce stress?

Note: This page reprinted with permission from William Shakespeare's *The Tempest*.

YOU MUST CHOOSE!

Would you... want to marry a creature who was half person/half couch?

Would you... attend a full season's games of the nearest WNBA team for a threesome with Erin Andrews and Anna Kournikova?

Would you... suckle from a nursing cow to suckle from Salma Hayek?

YOU MUST CHOOSE!

Date, Marry, Screw

Which would you date, which would you marry, and which would you screw?

Olivia Munn, Kathy Griffin, a mythical Griffin?
Jennifer Aniston, Courtney Cox, Megatron?

Things to consider: Aniston's legs, Cox's eyes, Megatron's desire for world domination and utter annihilation of the Autobots

Would you rather...

titty-fuck Jessica Rabbit
OR
fin-fuck the Little Mermaid?

YOU MUST CHOOSE!

Good Sports

Would you rather have sex with...

Danica Patrick **OR** Venus Williams?

an Olympic gymnast **OR** an Olympic figure skater?

tennis star Maria Sharapova grunting like she does when she plays **OR** hottie golf star Kim Hall as quiet as she is when she golfs?

a beach volleyball player covered in sand **OR** a pro bowler who celebrates upon orgasm like they would when they bowl a strike?

Things to consider: bowler's proclivity for instituting the Shocker, keeping score

Would you rather...

have your testicles set on a tee and hit by a five year old with a Wiffle bat

OR

have your testicles lowered between bumpers on a pinball machine?

YOU MUST CHOOSE!

Would you rather...

bang the *Sex in the City* characters in increasing order of sluttiness

OR

your choice of two panelists on *The View?*

Would you rather...

have sex with Lady Gaga

OR

with a few of her stage outfits?

YOU MUST CHOOSE!

Would you... toss the salad of your offensive linemen to be quarterback for a game in the NFL?

Would you... try to continue having sex with a very hot drunk woman if she threw up a little during sex? What would you say?

YOU MUST CHOOSE!

Would you rather...

plant an herb garden with Mandy Moore

OR

ride a freight train with Katherine Heigl?

Would you rather...

have group sex with the Pussycat Dolls

OR

the Spice Girls in their prime?

Would you rather...

have sex with Jennifer Lopez with H1N1

OR

let Jennifer Garner give you butterfly kisses with pinkeye?

YOU MUST CHOOSE!

Would you rather...

have Wolverine-type retractable claws made of penises

OR

not?

Would you rather...

go to a bachelor party thrown by Kubla Khan

OR

by Jabba the Hut?

Things to consider: the Mongol Horde is a potential sausage fest, keg stands with Boba Fett

Would you rather...

have sex with Adele

OR

pop Megan Fox's back zits?

YOU MUST CHOOSE!

While you're having sex, would you rather your partner scream out...

"Make love to me." **OR** "Fuck me harder!!!"

"Have you ever done this before?" **OR** "Allahu Akbar!"?

"Treat me like a whore!" **OR** "Kibbles 'n Bits! Kibbles 'n Bits! I've got to get me some Kibbles 'n Bits!"?

Would you rather...

have one clean shot to hit on Mila Kunis

OR

one clean shot to the face of Ryan Seacrest?

YOU MUST CHOOSE!

Would you rather...

have a detachable penis

OR

a penis that vibrates on command?

Would you rather...

lick Courtney Love's vibrator

OR

Tom Selleck's moustache?

Would you rather...

eat two live baby hamsters

OR

have sex with (insert disgusting acquaintance)?

YOU MUST CHOOSE!

30

GROSS — GROVER CLEVELAND

We are trying a little experiment with this chapter. This chapter is segmented by alphabetical order. Here you'll find questions about the "gross," then we'll move on to the "grotesque," and finally, the chapter will culminate with questions concerning "Grover Cleveland."

Would you rather...

groom a volatile gorilla

OR

groom the dingleberries from Michael Moore's ass hair?

Would you rather...

be climbing up the ladder and feel something splatter

OR

be sliding into first and feel something burst?

Things to consider: diarrhea, uh-uh, diarrheah.

YOU MUST CHOOSE!

Would you rather...

throw up right into a fan

OR

lick the dead bugs off of a car windshield?

Would you rather...

take it in the crapper

OR

on the crapper?

Would you rather...

have a beetle crawl in and around your mouth for two minutes

OR

have an inch worm slowly inch up your left nostril and out your right nostril?

YOU MUST CHOOSE!

Would you rather...

drink a pint of lukewarm asparagus pee

OR

16 ounces of chilled ball sweat?

Would you rather...

use a live possum as a pillow each night

OR

use a pile of rolled-up dirty diapers?

YOU MUST CHOOSE!

Would you rather...

have a tongue made of hair

OR

hair made of tongues?

Would you rather...

drink a glass of ten-month-old-milkshake complete with green chunky goodness

OR

eat a bowl of rat tails n' cheese?

YOU MUST CHOOSE!

Would you rather...

sleep nightly in pajamas made of dentists' used gauze

OR

have to reach into a horse's ass every time you want the key to your home?

Would you rather...

feel compelled to greet people by licking their feet

OR

by intensely smelling their armpits?

YOU MUST CHOOSE!

Would you rather...

have zits that pop by themselves, squirting as much goo as there is in a ketchup packet

OR

have zits that crawl all over your face like little ants?

Would you rather...

get poison ivy under your eyelid

OR

on your tongue?

Would you rather...

eat chocolate-covered cockroaches

OR

deep-fried roadkill?

YOU MUST CHOOSE!

Would you rather...

eat a cow-eye-and-cricket shish kabob marinated in camel spit

OR

a salad of giant moth wings tossed in dog slobber dressing?

Would you rather...

get a hickey from each of your grandparents

OR

give them each one?

Would you rather...

get a mayonnaise enema

OR

eat a piece of bull-semen-iced angelfood cake?

YOU MUST CHOOSE!

Would you rather...

hold a slug on your tongue for two hours

OR

get a bee sting on your sphincter?

Would you rather...

eat a regurgitated cat hairball

OR

pasta boiled in used toilet water?

YOU MUST CHOOSE!

Would you rather...

lick clean the inside of a horse's nostril

OR

have a horse lick the insides of your nostril?

Would you rather...

play basketball against a gross, flabby, hairy, shirtless, sweaty old dude

OR

play tackle football against a 300 pounder?

YOU MUST CHOOSE!

Would you rather...

have your body hair suddenly turn into fleas

OR

have your saliva suddenly turn into glue?

Would you rather...

eat a cotton candy that turns out to be a cocoon full of caterpillars

OR

that turned out to be an old man's whitened pubic hair?

YOU MUST CHOOSE!

Would you rather...

have bloodworms for facial hair

OR

use facial hair for fishing bait? (work in progress)

Would you rather...

after sneezing, use a piece of used tissue

OR

just use your shirt?

YOU MUST CHOOSE!

Would you rather...

have projectile vomit

OR

have projectile diarrhea?

Would you rather...

have an infestation of bedbugs

OR

bed Larry Kings?

Would you rather...

lose control of your bowels upon orgasm

OR

vice-versa?

YOU MUST CHOOSE!

Would you rather...

have your horror-movie death involve a chainsaw **OR** a meat hook?

ice pick **OR** toothpicks?

The Count from *Sesame Street* **OR** Wolfgang Puck?

Would you rather...

be thrown up on while giving

OR

receiving oral sex?

YOU MUST CHOOSE!

Would you rather...

wear used urinal cake ear muffs

OR

brush with smegma toothpaste?

Would you rather...

drop a Mentos in a glass of Diet Coke and immediately take a swig

OR

have an enema of the same?

Would you rather...

drink a maggot smoothie

OR

bathe in the thick gooey fat drained from Hollywood actress's liposuction treatments?

YOU MUST CHOOSE!

Would you rather...

have a lawnmower run over a cow patty and spatter you with its smelly chopped-up bits

OR

have to clean out a soiled hamster's cage with your bare hands?

Would you rather...

breathe through your navel

OR

through your butt?

Things to consider: snorkeling, wearing baggy pants to give you some breathing room, if you have an outie or innie

YOU MUST CHOOSE!

Would you rather...
shove a straw into a big blister and suck away

OR

eat a sherbet-sized scoop of ear wax?

Would you rather...
eat raw cow stomach

OR

stomach 500 cow farts in a row, standing 2 inches behind the cow?

Would you rather...
eat a Twinkie filled with human blood

OR

eat a Nutty Buddy rolled in dingleberries?

YOU MUST CHOOSE!

If you were Grover Cleveland, would you rather...

intervene in the Pullman Strike of 1894 to keep the railroads moving, thereby angering labor unions nationwide

OR

support the gold standard and oppose free silver thereby alienating the agrarian wing of the Democratic Party?

Would you rather...

be haunted by the ghosts of Grover Cleveland's appointed Supreme Court justices Lucius Q.C. Lamar and Melville Fuller

OR

have nightmares where you are being attacked by Grover Cleveland's mustache?

YOU MUST CHOOSE!

Would you... have a three-way with Grover Cleveland and vice-president Adlai Stevenson to reverse their stance on the 15th amendment, guaranteeing rights for African Americans?

YOU MUST CHOOSE!

CHAPTER THIRTY-ONE

31

RANDOM/"RANDOM"

If you like the weird, "random" questions full of obscure references, mad-libby nonsense and strange juxtapositions, then this chapter is for you. If, on the other hand, you prefer more straightforward mainstream material, please turn to page 184. Of another book.

Would you rather...

have perpetual helium voice

OR

shake your head knowingly and say "Old School!" after anything
a person you meet for the first time says during conversation?

Would you rather...

have a rare condition where you assume all police officers you see
are coming after you

OR

coming on to you?

Would you rather...

no matter what, always be wearing a leopard skin and holding a club

OR

no matter what, always be holding a knife and wearing
blood-soaked clothing?

Things to consider: walks in the park, grocery shopping,
parent teacher conferences

YOU MUST CHOOSE!

Would you rather...

have phantom phone syndrome where you constantly think your phone vibrates even when it doesn't

OR

have phantom yarmulke syndrome?

Would you rather...

be a brilliant songwriter, but only get inspired after making out with former Secretary of State Madeleine Albright

OR

have keen foresight about the stock market, but only while fondling a head of lettuce in public?

YOU MUST CHOOSE!

Would you rather...

have eyelids that are always flipped up

OR

have all of your skin be wrinkly, scraggly-haired scrotum skin?

Would you rather...

have a rare speech impediment where your lips and voice are out of sync like a '70s kung fu movie

OR

have an air horn blast the second you are not sitting with perfect posture?

Would you rather...

wink flirtatiously after every sentence

OR

be mentally sound in every way, except completely unable to use faucets?

YOU MUST CHOOSE!

Would you rather...

have to solve a SuDoKu before being able to open the refrigerator

OR

before being allowed to go home from work, have to draw 100 high-fives from different strangers?

Would you rather...

only be able to urinate while reciting the pledge of allegiance

OR

have an acid flashback of the Vietnam War anytime anyone says "facetious"?

YOU MUST CHOOSE!

Would you rather...

have to legally change your name to "Lelsdy" **OR** "Trongar"?

"The (insert your name here)" **OR** "(insert your name here) of the Mountain People"?

the sound of a glass shattering **OR** the smell of vanilla?

Would you rather...

only be able to communicate with people via singing telegram

OR

singing anagram?

YOU MUST CHOOSE!

Would you rather...

have a rectum that can sing like Frank Sinatra

OR

a vagina with the sardonic wit of Bea Arthur?

Would you rather...

have to drink everything via keg stand

OR

from a thimble-sized glass?

YOU MUST CHOOSE!

Would you rather...

stare fixedly at people's nostrils when speaking to them

OR

sob uncontrollably anytime you use the ATM?

Would you rather...

have to get a new plastic surgery procedure every month

OR

have to get a new tattoo every day?

YOU MUST CHOOSE!

Would you rather...

only be able to talk to the opposite sex in '70s jive

OR

like Gollum from *Lord of the Rings*?

Would you rather...

have the ability to telekinetically control anyone's arms

OR

anyone's hair?

Would you rather...

burp fireflies

OR

fart smooth jazz?

YOU MUST CHOOSE!

Would you rather...

never be able take off your underwear

OR

a catcher's mitt?

Would you rather...

in all photographs, appear as Sam Waterson

OR

uncontrollably shriek every time you see argyle?

YOU MUST CHOOSE!

Would you rather...

have 8 ears **OR** 36 nostrils?

10 eyes **OR** 24 fingers?

400 lips **OR** 8000 toes?

Would you rather...

recite famous historical speeches in your sleep

OR

perform various swim strokes in your sleep?

YOU MUST CHOOSE!

Would you rather have sex with the hybrid...

Ashley Judd Nelson **OR** Sarah Jessica Parker Posey?

Keri Russell Brand **OR** Lil' Kim Jong-il?

Selma Blair Underwood **OR** Ricky Martin Heidegger?

YOU MUST CHOOSE!

Would you rather...

be completely unable to detect sarcasm

OR

be the totally awesome reader that we *really* care about even though this is the fifteenth year of writing this stuff that doesn't bore us at all any more?

Would you rather be able to move with your mind...

bowling pins **OR** motorcycles?

cauliflower **OR** worms?

silverware **OR** chalk?

Things to consider: how would you use your powers?

YOU MUST CHOOSE!

Would you rather...

speak as if you are always out of breath

OR

speak as if you were using an auto tuner (the thing that makes singers sound robotic)?

Would you rather...

when eating, shift into slow motion

OR

speak like a wise Native American chief whenever you're chilly?

Would you rather...

sneeze a blast of shotgun pellets

OR

always look like you are crying with tons of makeup smearing?

Things to consider: the angle of your head when sneezing, the kick-back of a sneeze, kissing

YOU MUST CHOOSE!

Would you rather...

not be able to tell the difference between keys and Q-tips

OR

guns and celery?

Would you rather...

have tennis ball-sized eyeballs

OR

coffee mug-sized nostrils?

YOU MUST CHOOSE!

Would you rather...

be unable to stop from tackling anyone over 75-years-old

OR

grow a bushy beard every day on a different part of your body?

Things to consider: visiting a retirement home, knee-beards, foot beards, forehead beards

Would you rather...

have extra eyeballs in the palms of your hands

OR

detachable ears that you can leave anywhere and work like walkie-talkies?

Would you rather...

have a goatee (ring of hair) around each eye

OR

have earlobes that connect under your chin?

YOU MUST CHOOSE!

Would you rather...

have poppy-seeded skin

OR

have asparagus for hair?

Would you rather...

say the word "whitefish" every other word as in: "Hi whitefish, how whitefish, have whitefish you whitefish been?"

OR

have a strange condition where anytime you walk into a room, dozens of pickles fall on your head?

YOU MUST CHOOSE!

Would you rather...

only be able to enter rooms by Kool-Aid-man-style wall crashes

OR

only be able to exit rooms by jumping through a window as if fleeing a burning building?

Would you rather...

have baby-sized feet

OR

baby-sized hands?

Things to consider: sports, writing, toppling, finding shoes

Would you rather...

be able to shoot mustard from your eyes

OR

be able to extend one eyeball up, out and around corners like a submarine periscope?

YOU MUST CHOOSE!

Would you rather...

have glow-in-the-dark poops

OR

dimes for boogers?

Would you rather...

have to battle a blindfolded Bengal tiger **OR** 600 yipping poodles?

a 5x scale Betty White **OR** a 1/5x Chuck Norris?

your own left hand **OR** your own right foot?

Would you rather...

all family functions and celebrations be held in an ATM vestibule

OR

catered exclusively by the bourbon chicken free sample guy
from the mall food court?

YOU MUST CHOOSE!

Would you rather...

be getting busy with someone for the first time, and as you take their pants off, you see they have the largest amount of pubic hair you have ever seen

OR

you see a crotch tattoo of Matlock?

Would you rather have all your future dreams consist of...

being naked in high school **OR** of taking a test you forgot to study for?

being surrounded by lingerie-wearing Richard Nixon clones **OR** playing Parcheesi with a temperamental Charles Barkley?

being trapped in a passionless marriage to Eli Whitney **OR** being sexually harassed by Oliver Wendell Holmes?

YOU MUST CHOOSE!

Would you rather...

look like this

OR

look like this?

YOU MUST CHOOSE!

WHAT WOULD YOU BE?

How to Use This Chapter

Game 1: I Am Thinking of Someone We All Know. This is a way to use this chapter as a group game. One player thinks of someone who everybody in the group knows: a friend, a coworker, an enemy, a teacher, etc. This is the "name on the table." Other players take turns reading a randomly selected page of questions from this chapter. The player who is thinking of someone answers each question as if he were that person. After every page, have a player guess who you are thinking of. Optional: If you want, you can all write down a bunch of people you know on scraps of paper, turn them over, and have the answerer pull a name from the pile.

Game 2: Conversation. Pretty simple. Read a question and answer it as yourself. If there is a group of you, everybody should answer the question. Suggest your own answers for what you think others are and discuss why. See who agrees and who disagrees. Debate. Deliberate. Arm-wrestle. Think about other people you know (your friends, family, bosses, etc.) and what they would be. When the conversation fades into silence and awkward stares—you guessed it—it's time to move on to the next question.

Game 3: Celebrity. Go back a page. Reread the directions for Game 1, but substitute "celebrity" for "someone who everybody in the group knows."

Game 4: Ninja Strike. Find a horde of bandits marauding caravans. Train in the martial arts, specializing in book warfare. Fashion this book into a throwing star or other deadly piece of weaponry. Defeat marauders.

If you were a **company**, what would you be?

If you were **something that goes in the mouth**, what would you be?

If you were a **cooking technique** (grilling, broiling, slow-cook, etc.), what would you be?

If you were any **palindrome** (race car, mom, dad, etc.), what would you be?

YOU MUST CHOOSE!

Your True Character

If you were a **character** from *Harry Potter*, who would you be?

If you were a **character** from *Lost*, who would you be?

If you were a **character** from *True Blood*, who would you be?

If you were a **character** from *Sex and the City*, who would you be?

If you were a **character** from *Grey's Anatomy*, who would you be?

YOU MUST CHOOSE!

If you were a Starbucks order, what would you be? (Give a detailed order.)
Things to consider: Are you decaf? Skim? Size? Iced? Latte?

If you were a jungle animal, what would you be?

If you were a kind of massage, what would you be? (Demonstrate if needed.)
Things to consider: Would you be forceful? Gentle? An erotic massage? A neurotic massage?

Question of character

Would you ever give or receive a "happy ending" massage? A happy beginning? A melancholy middle?

YOU MUST CHOOSE!

If you were a **tree**, what would you be?

If you were a **coin**, which coin would you be?

If you were a **piece of gardening equipment**, what would you be?

If you were any **alien as depicted in science fiction**, what would you be?
Things to consider: the ferocious creature in *Alien*, the seemingly benign but ultimately evil reptiles from *V*, Jawas, the ultralogical *Star Trek* super-race susceptible to being defeated by paradox.

YOU MUST CHOOSE!

Setting the Bar

If you were a type of bar, what would you be?
Describe your:
Décor and lighting?

Clientele? What sort of conversations do they have? Are there fights?

What do you serve? What sort of neighborhood are you located in?

What music is playing? Any other details?

What are you named?

YOU MUST CHOOSE!

If you were a **character from** *Peanuts*, who would you be?

Things to consider: Are you balding? Do you neglect your personal hygiene to the point of being a health hazard? Do you need a security blanket? Are you a Butch lesbian? Do you hold things out for people and suddenly take them away?

If you were a **foreign language**, what would you be?

If you were an **obscene gesture**, what would you be?
(Demonstration optional.)

If you were a **period in history**, which period would you be?

YOU MUST CHOOSE!

QUIZ

Who is this famous person?

If he were an animal, he might be a hyena. Though a few would claim he is a lion.

If he were a weapon, he'd be a whip or maybe a Colt 45.

If he were a tool, he'd be a hammer.

If he were a key on the keyboard, detractors would say he'd be the Delete key. Supporters would say he's the Enter key.

If he were a punctuation mark, he'd be an exclamation mark.

Answer: George W. Bush

YOU MUST CHOOSE!

If you were a **road sign**, what would you be?

YOU MUST CHOOSE!

If you were a **reptile or amphibian**, what would you be?

If you were a **commercial slogan** ("Just Do It", "Sometimes you feel like a nut…", "I'm not gonna pay a lot for this muffler…", "Keeps on going and going and going…", etc.), what would you be?

If you were a **character from _Friends_**, which would you be?

If you were an **over-the-counter medication**, what would you be?

Did you know?

*Matt LeBlanc has two club feet.**

*Not true.

YOU MUST CHOOSE!

Web You.0

If you were a **website**, what would you be?

If you were a **download speed**, what would you be? Does your connection go out a lot?

If you were a **spider web**, what would you look like? Draw it. What if Charlotte from *Charlotte's Web* made a web to represent you?

Question of character

If you started typing "po..." in a web browser, what is most likely to pop up from frequent use: popsugar.com, pornocentral.com, or polygonsrcool.net? Check your browser and see.

YOU MUST CHOOSE!

If you were a **Monopoly property** (Boardwalk, Baltic Avenue, etc.), what would you be?

If you were an **extinct animal**, what would you be?

If you were a **number between one and ten**, what number would you be?

Things to consider: What number gets laid the most? What number is the biggest asshole? What is the most beautiful number? The most mysterious? The most pelborp?

If you were an **item in the supermarket**, what would you be?

Question of character

What are the **first five items** on your shopping list?

What would never be on it?

YOU MUST CHOOSE!

Are you...

Meat, chicken, or fish?

87, 89, or 93 gasoline?

Boxers, briefs, or nothing?

Firemen, police, or paramedics?

a shot, assist, or rebound?

YOU MUST CHOOSE!

If you were **something in a yard**, what would you be?

If you were **something in a mall**, what would you be?

If you were **something in Washington, D.C.**, what would you be?

If you were **something in the closet**, what would you be?

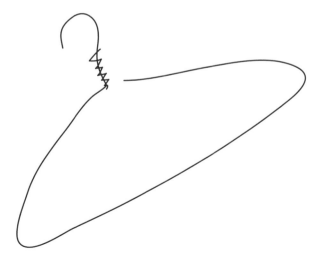

YOU MUST CHOOSE!

Who's the Boss?

If your boss were a **movie villain**, which one would he/she be?

If your boss were an **amusement park ride**, which one would he/she be?

If your boss were a **piece of email spam**, what would the subject line say?

If your boss were a **tourist attraction**, which would he/she be?

YOU MUST CHOOSE!

Are you …

a **consonant** or a **vowel**?

a **thrust** or a **parry**?

Bert or **Ernie**?

Dr. Jekyll or **Mr. Hyde**?

a **whisper** or a **shout**?

YOU MUST CHOOSE!

Fantasy Football

If you were a **position in football**, what would you be?

If you were a **football play** (sack, touchdown, reverse, blocked punt, Hail Mary, etc.), which would you be? Bonus: Do the commentary of four downs that embody your life.

If you were an **NFL team**, what team would you be and why? Examples: A Bengal—good-looking uniform (body), ugly helmet (face).

If you were a **football penalty**, what would you be?

Question of character

If you had to do a **post-touchdown celebration** that personifies you, what would you do? (Demonstrate it.)

YOU MUST CHOOSE!

If you were a **song from the early eighties**, what song would you be?

If you were a **cut of steak**, what cut would you be? How would you be cooked? Seasoned?

If you were a **sitcom character**, who would you be?

Question of character

If you had an **original sitcom catchphrase**, what would it be? Some ideas: … "Uh, NO THANK YOU!"; "That's a little more info than I need to knooooowwwwwwwww!"; "Guess you had to be there"; "Indeeditron 2000!"; and "Sheeeeeyit!"

YOU MUST CHOOSE!

Sumpin' Sumpin'

If you were **something with wheels**, what would you be?

If you were **something with wings**, what would you be?

If you were **something on a farm**, what would you be?

If you were **something in the kitchen**, what would you be?

Things to consider: Can you think of an object that satisfies all of the above? If so, email the answer to info@sevenfooter.com, subject heading: "Too much time on my balls." So far, the best we have is a partially formed chicken in an egg (but no wheels).

YOU MUST CHOOSE!

If you were a **Disney character**, what would you be?

If you were a **gun**, what would you be?

If you were a **mythical creature**, what would you be?

If you were an **architectural style**, what would you be?

Question of character

If *Disney on Ice* put on an **ice show of your life**, how would that go?

YOU MUST CHOOSE!

If you were a **mode of transportation**,
what would you be?

If you were an **email command**, what would you be?
Things to consider: reply, forward, delete, archive, send, keep as new

If you were a **store**, what would you be?

If you were a **magic spell**, what would you be?
Things to consider; invisibility, forcefield, fireball, freeze, levitate, turn to stone,
poison, prismatic lights, cure wounds.

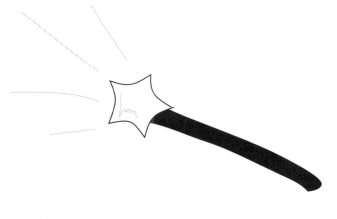

YOU MUST CHOOSE!

If you were a **disease**, what would you be?

If you were a **culture from history** (Aztec, Vikings, Cherokee, etc.), what would you be?

If you were a **bumper sticker**, what would you be?

If you were a **button on your TV remote**, what would you be?

YOU MUST CHOOSE!

20 Stupid Questions

Take a break from WWYB to play this game. If in a public place, pick someone you don't know, but that each of you can see. If not in a public place, think of a well-known celebrity or historical figure. Then play 20 questions, but use only these questions of conjecture. One player pick the person, the other ask. After asking/answering these questions, guess who the person is. Indeeditron 2000.

- Could you see this person secretly liking to be tied up and dominated?

- Does this person misspell "maintenance"?

- If this person was in a fight with Tom Bergeron, would they win?

- Is this person a farter?

- Does this person sing in the shower? On the toilet?

- Does he/she have a good voice?

- Does this person like penguins?

- Do these pants make my butt look big? My balls?

YOU MUST CHOOSE!

If you were a **donut**, what would you be? What if you were a doughnut?

If you were a **president**, who would you be?

If you were a **decade**, which decade would you be?

If you were a **TV channel**, what would you be?

Did you know?

John Quincy Adams was the world's first bisexual.*

*Not true.

YOU MUST CHOOSE!

If you were a kiss, what would you be?
(Demonstrate on your hand.)

If you were foreplay, what would you be?
(Demonstrate on your forearm.)

If you were a form of sexual intercourse, what would you be? (Demonstrate on the throw pillow or couch corner.)

Question of character

What is the weirdest sexual dream you've ever had?

YOU MUST CHOOSE!

If you were a **beer**, what would you be?

If you were an **occupation**, what would you be?

If you were a **height**, which one would you be?

If you were a **drunken antic**, what would you be?
Act it out.

Things to consider: being over-friendly, getting into a fight, dropping pants, talking too much like Loose Lips Schirtz.

YOU MUST CHOOSE!

If you were a **basketball shot**, what would you be? (Examples: short-range jump hook, two-handed tomahawk dunk, fade-away 3-pointer)? Does your shot go in?

If you were a **famous singer**, who would you be?

If you were a **school supply**, what would you be?

If you were a **dance style**, what would you be (tap, break-dancing, ballet, square-dancing, etc.)?

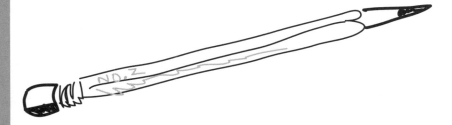

YOU MUST CHOOSE!

Acting Out

If you were a **talent show act**, what would it be?
(Demonstrate it.)

If you were a **'70s song**, which would it be?
(Sing it.)

If you were a **quote from a movie**, what would it be?
(Say it.)

If you were a **scene from a movie**, which would it be?
(Mime it.)

YOU MUST CHOOSE!

If you were a **street**, what would you be?

If you were a **fashion accessory**, what would you be?

If you were a **soda**, what would you be?

If you were a **classic arcade game character**, what would you be?

Things to consider: Are you a glutton that loves the thrill of the chase? Do you have a hero streak and a propensity to dodge barrels either literally or metaphorically? Are you prone to diagonal hopping and unidentifiably punctuated profanity?

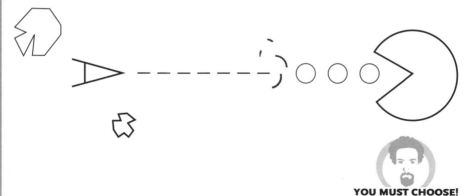

YOU MUST CHOOSE!

If you were a **fashion label**, which one would you be?

If you were a **restaurant chain**, which would you be?

If you were a **part of speech**, which would you be?

If you were a **spread that you put on bread** (mayonnaise, margarine, peanut butter, Vegemite, marshmallow fluff, *etc.*), what would you be?

YOU MUST CHOOSE!

CHAPTER THIRTY-THREE

33

FANTASIES

Albert Einstein once said, "The gift of fantasy has meant more to me than my talent for absorbing positive knowledge." Consequently, Einstein was a profound and constant masturbator, which very few people realize. His productivity would have been twice what it was if he could manage to stave off his flooding fantasies. But we cannot deny the dreaming mind. As human beings, we must feed it. And so we present to you these choices in the far-off, far-out realms of fantasy. Choose wisely (unlike Einstein).

Would you rather...

be allowed to destroy Lego Land, pretending you are a giant monster

OR

be allowed to have a paintball war in your office?

Would you rather...

have Yoda as your personal bodyguard

OR

as your (or your child's) school guidance counselor?

Would you rather...

watch Britney Spears and Christina Aguilera in a UFC match-up

OR

watch Dick Cheney and Hillary Clinton?

YOU MUST CHOOSE!

Would you rather...

have a star on the Hollywood Walk of Fame

OR

have a deli sandwich named after you?

Would you rather...

be slapped by an ugly girl

OR

thrown up on by a hot girl?

Would you rather...

have an element on the periodic chart renamed after you

OR

have a new hit dance based on your movement style sweep the country?

YOU MUST CHOOSE!

Would you rather...

make a frittata with Philip Seymour Hoffman

OR

play Mastermind with Clint Eastwood?

Would you rather...

go to a strip club where all the strippers are crushes you had in high school

OR

a strip club where all the strippers say what they are actually thinking?

Would you rather...

once a day, feel the sensation of a good orgasm

OR

feel the feeling you got when you were a kid and you awoke to find it snowing outside and that school was cancelled?

YOU MUST CHOOSE!

Date, Screw, Kill

Which of the three would you date, which would you screw, and which would you kill?

Heidi Montag, Taylor Swift, Aunt Jemima

Hulk Hogan, Donald Trump, Mario from video game fame

Jonah Hill, Michael Cera, Simon Cowell

Tin Man, Scarecrow, Cowardly Lion

Things to consider: giving your heart to the Tin Man, screwing your brains out with the Scarecrow, the Cowardly Lion = gay?

YOU MUST CHOOSE!

Would you rather...

be able to make anyone you touch have perfect 6 pack abs

OR

have an IQ of 140?

Would you rather never get...

tired **OR** hungry?

B.O. **OR** gas?

called "Dorkazon 2000" **OR** hit in the head with a pineapple?

Would you rather...

have sex with Zachary Quinto's Spock

OR

Leonard Nimoy's?

YOU MUST CHOOSE!

Back that App Up!

Would you rather...

have an app that tells you the size of a man's junk upon meeting him **OR** that translates what a guy is saying to what he is actually thinking?

an app that tells you how far a prospective date is willing to go **OR** that functions as birth control if you shine it on your privates for 30 seconds?

that works as a mirror **OR** as a throwing star?

YOU MUST CHOOSE!

Your most attractive friends invite you and your partner to have group sex. Would you rather participate or not?

Would you rather always be age...

5 **OR** 35?

12 **OR** 50?

2 **OR** 62?

YOU MUST CHOOSE!

Which would you rather use as an erotic food to enhance sex...

whipped cream **OR** melted chocolate?

A-1 sauce **OR** hard-boiled eggs?

Fun Dip **OR** gobstoppers?

Would you rather...

have sex with a "5"

OR

have sex with a "3" while a "10" watches?

YOU MUST CHOOSE!

Would you rather...

get a fifteen minute shopping spree (whatever you grab you keep)
in Dress Barn

OR

in a Macy's with a loose Siberian tiger?

Would you rather...

have an extra set of your gender's genitals anywhere you choose
on your body

OR

have the addition of the opposite gender's genitals on your body?

Things to consider: three-ways, one-ways, rainy days

YOU MUST CHOOSE!

Would you rather...

have your office's water cooler filled with malt liquor

OR

have Extremely Casual Friday (where everyone wears Daisy Duke shorts)?

Would you rather...

have access to live webcams of every room in the White House

OR

every room in your neighbors' houses?

YOU MUST CHOOSE!

Would you rather...

play video games for a job but make only minimum wage

OR

be a peep show booth cleaner and make $100,000 a year?

Would you rather...

live on the International Space Station for a month **OR** on a tropical island?

live in a planetarium **OR** an amusement park?

on a tugboat **OR** in a ranch home with Phil Jackson?

Would you rather...

change the National Anthem to "Pants on the Ground" (made famous on *American Idol*)

OR

change the words to the Pledge of Allegiance to the "Diarrhea Song"?

Things to consider: Place your hand over your heart and try both.

YOU MUST CHOOSE!

Would you rather...

watch your parents have a freestyle rap battle

OR

watch your parents have a freestyle dance battle?

Would you rather...

get to play "Truth or Dare" with famous celebrities

OR

famous historical figures?
Who would you choose to play with?
What would you ask them as a Truth?
What would dare them to do?

YOU MUST CHOOSE!

Would you rather...

have a kangaroo butler

OR

a monkey chauffeur?

Would you rather...

get ahead in life using your mind **OR** looks?

your connections **OR** your hard work?

your low post moves **OR** *Saved by The Bell* trivia knowledge?

Would you rather...

get to be a guest judge on *American Idol*

OR

get to force one of your friends to go on it?

YOU MUST CHOOSE!

Would you rather...

have a kitchen designed by the people that make James Bond contraptions

OR

a bike designed by them?

Would you rather...

win a Grammy **OR** an Oscar?

a pro sport's MVP prize **OR** the Nobel Peace Prize?

a bocce tournament in front of a bunch of hot chicks **OR** a Pro-Am charity golf tournament in front of no one?

YOU MUST CHOOSE!

Would you rather...

have your parents go on *Dancing with the Stars* **OR** *America's Got Talent?*

The Biggest Loser **OR** *What Not to Wear?*

The Apprentice **OR** *Top Chef?*

Would you rather...

get around by hovercraft

OR

pterodactyl?

Would you rather...

play Simon Says with Samuel L. Jackson

OR

go bowling with Michael Richards?

YOU MUST CHOOSE!

WORLD'S BEST
VENEREAL DISEASES

Which of the following would you most want to have?

Genital diamonds

Sexually Transmitted MP3's

The Clap-on/Clap-off Clap

Vaginal ATM

Free Carpool Lane Gonorrhea

YOU MUST CHOOSE!

Which would you rather use as a sex toy...

a snuggie **OR** a menorah?

a wiffle ball **OR** a hand saw?

a cafeteria tray **OR** a credenza?

Would you rather...

have access to a Facebook for sex, where you can log in and see everyone your friends have had sex with, your friends' friends, the whole world interlocking in six degrees of separation

OR

not?

Would you rather...

play backgammon with Mandy Moore

OR

make popsicle crafts with Michelle Rodriguez?

YOU MUST CHOOSE!

Would you rather...

ride shotgun in a NASCAR race

OR

eliminate NASCAR from the planet?

Would you rather...

have a retractable ball-point pen in your finger

OR

have a laser pointer finger?

Would you rather...

have every part of your body be as pleasure-sensitive as your genitals

OR

not?

YOU MUST CHOOSE!

Would you rather live in a world where...

when dining at a restaurant, your laundry is done while you eat **OR** where all professional and doctor waiting rooms have a free, full-time masseuse?

Would you rather live in a world where...

much like episodes of *Sesame Street*, the corporate sponsor of every TV show is a letter/number

OR

where people vacation only by assuming the identities of others?

YOU MUST CHOOSE!

Would you rather live in a world where...

every person had a photographic memory

OR

x-ray vision?

Would you rather live in a world where...

animals had the same rights as people

OR

where animals had ketchup, mustard, and barbecue sauce in their blood?

YOU MUST CHOOSE!

MORE WOULD YOU...?

"Everybody has a price… for the million dollar man."
—D.H. Lawrence

There's no such thing as a free lunch. Unless you feign interest in buying foods at Whole Foods where they are serving up free samples. That's it though: free samples at Whole Foods. Or I guess if you go to an art opening and eat all the cocktail food pretending to be interested in the art. But that's it: art openings and Whole Foods free samples. That's all. And wakes. You don't pay for wakes. Okay, so there are lots of free lunches. But not in this case. Here, there is a price to pay for whatever it is that you want.

Would you... get one DD breast implant for $900,000?

Would you... punch your grandmother in the stomach in order to get free cable for the rest of your life?

Would you... watch your parents have sex thrice to end world hunger?

Would you... Dutch-oven a 4-year-old orphan for an extra week's vacation at school/work?

Would you... sleep with the ugliest person at school/work (with no repercussions) for a promotion?

YOU MUST CHOOSE!

Panda-Monium

Would you... mate with a panda if it meant saving 50 pandas every time you did it? How many times would you mate?

Would you... stop funding panda efforts and let nature take its course and have the panda go extinct?

Would you... hunt and kill 50 pandas with a bow and arrow to be able to have sex whenever and with whomever you choose?

YOU MUST CHOOSE!

Would you... lose an inch of height to gain two inches of length? (Women: "have your partner...")

Would you... berate an old woman for no reason for fifteen minutes in a closet with Jessica Alba? (Women: receive oral from Johnny Depp)?

Would you... drink forty bottles of ketchup in a row for $50,000?

YOU MUST CHOOSE!

Would you... remove your pants in public to establish a free WiFi hotspot?

Would you... sucker-punch your boss if there were absolutely no negative repercussions?

Would you... sleep your way up the ladder if you were attractive enough to pull it off? How about down the ladder if you're not?

Would you... love the one you're with if you can't be with the one you love?

YOU MUST CHOOSE!

743

Would you... have sex with Susan Boyle to have sex with Brooke Burke?

Would you... lick peanut butter off a dog's balls for your choice of season tickets to your favorite team or yearly Oscar tickets?

Would you... put on 70 pounds for a movie role? For $10,000? For the hell of it?

Would you... allow your wife or husband to make out with and feverishly grope a stranger one time in order to lower your mortgage interest rate by 1%?

YOU MUST CHOOSE!

Would you... screw Megan Fox/Brad Pitt if you knew a random person in the world would die because of it?

Would you... engage in heavy petting with Zac Efron in order to ensure there are no more *High School Musical* movies ever made again?

Would you... shoot seltzer water into the face of a homeless person in order to sleep with your choice of Taylor Lautner/ Alyssa Milano?

YOU MUST CHOOSE!

For the Ladies

Would you... screw Hugh Jackman if it gave you shingles?

Would you... shave Alan Alda's balls for $500 a ball? Would you do both or just one?

Would you... date Mike Tyson for $1,000 a day? How many days would you last?

YOU MUST CHOOSE!

No one likes it when actors and actresses get mixed up in politics. Nonetheless, which of the following would you do?

Would you have sex with...

Hillary Clinton to get to have sex with your choice of Hilary Swank or Hilary Duff?

former Mexican President Vicente Fox to get to have sex with Megan Fox?

late Senator Strom Thurmond for Uma Thurman?

Jesse Jackson for Janet Jackson?

Michael Moore for your choice of Mandy or Demi Moore?

YOU MUST CHOOSE!

Would you... let Iron Chef Bobby Flay cook all your meals if it meant having to share a sleeping bag with him every night?

Would you... take an all-expense-paid vacation to Europe if you had to travel the whole time in a World War II motorcycle sidecar with Flavor Flav?

Would you... French kiss your pet for $100?

YOU MUST CHOOSE!

Public Privates

Would you... slyly masturbate to completion
on a public bus for $10,000?

at your office desk for $15,000?

in a Radio Shack from $18,000?

during a haircut for $35,000?

at a funeral for $50,000?

YOU MUST CHOOSE!

Would you... spend a month in space if it meant having to share the space station with the cast of *Jersey Shore*?

Would you... have one droopy eye if it meant being irresistibly attractive to librarians?

Would you... attend a stranger's wedding, vehemently claiming an ongoing relationship with the groom as well as the grandmother of the bride for $5000?

YOU MUST CHOOSE!

Would you... crash a funeral wearing fanatical sports fan attire (face paint, rainbow wig, posterboard using bold network letters in a contrived statement like "**E**ulogies **S**upport **P**allbearers' **N**otions," etc.) to stave off your own death for an extra two years?

Would you... perform a *Vagina Monologue*-esque rendition about your own genitalia to a packed theater for $10,000? How about a Diarrhea Monolouge where you recount your best stories of self-defecation?

Would you... legally change your name to Osama Bin Laden for $600,000 and a spelunking trip to Pakistan?

YOU MUST CHOOSE!

Would you... receive a pearl necklace from Artie Lange if it turned into a real, high-quality pearl necklace? If this continued to happen, how many times would you engage?

Would you... administer reciprocal blumpkins with World Wrestling Entertainment's Mark Henry for $2 million?

Would you... spend a weekend having sex with Eva Mendes, if you had a 49% chance of catching genital warts?

Would you... dump your current friends to be best friends with (insert some celebrity?)

YOU MUST CHOOSE!

Would you... take half Bill Gates' fortune but have to be four times as nerdy?

Would you... get caught taking a dump on your neighbors' living room rug for free cell phone service?

Would you... eat a dog to save yours from being eaten?

Would you... live for a year in a fort you built when you were 9-years-old to live in your dream house for the following year?

YOU MUST CHOOSE!

Would you...
have sex with this guy

OR
this guy ?

YOU MUST CHOOSE!

Serious Questions

Would you... give up sex for monk-like wisdom and calm of mind?

Would you... never have sex again for world peace?

Would you... punch a rabbi in the nose in order to get a BJ from Taylor Swift?

YOU MUST CHOOSE!

Would you... have a three way with Optimus Prime and Megatron to peacefully resolve the long-standing war between Decepticons and Autobots?

Would you... do Tyler Perry in drag for 1/100th of his wealth?

Would you... become a vegan for a year for a threesome with Natalie Portman and Zooey Deschanel?

Would you... miss a year of life with your partner in order to relive your senior year of college?

YOU MUST CHOOSE!

To have sex with your celebrity crush, would you...

consume a bottle of mayonnaise in ten minutes?

poop in your pants for a week?

carry a ladle around at all times in public for a year?

increase global temperature 1 degree immediately, drastically worsening global warming?

step on and squash a baby chick?

YOU MUST CHOOSE!

To have sex with your celebrity crush, would you...

eat 15 bull testicles?

not wear deodorant for a year?

get a genital piercing that has your keys attached to it?

change you legal name permanently to "Prelnar"?

sneak up behind you mom, and knock her legs out from under her?

YOU MUST CHOOSE!

Would you...

have sex with this woman

to have sex with this one?

YOU MUST CHOOSE!

CHAPTER **35** THIRTY-FIVE

PRIVILEGES AND POSSESSIONS

Lucky you. The good times continue to roll. For reasons beyond your understanding, you are either being granted a prized possession (an object, creature, or person of great possibility) or a precious privilege (an honor, convenience, or enticing opportunity). What you do with your newfound blessing is up to you, as is the choice between two equally awesome options.

Would you rather...

have your face carved into Mt. Rushmore

OR

have your ass carved into Mt. Rushmore?

Who would you rather have in your camp at Burning Man?

ventriloquist Jeff Dunham **OR** Al Roker?

Johnny Depp from *Pirates of the Caribbean* **OR** Johnny Depp from *Alice in Wonderland*?

Socrates **OR** Fozzie Bear?

Marilyn Manson and Charles Manson **OR** the Dalai Lama and Dolly Parton?

YOU MUST CHOOSE!

Would you rather...

have a Real Sex Doll in the likeness of Jenna Haze **OR** Wonder Woman?

an anonymous hot woman **OR** the celebrity of your choice?

Harriet Tubman **OR** a hot Klingon woman?

Would you rather...

have a huge table-top iPad (à la table-top Pac Man at Pizza Hut)
OR
a Bluetooth head?

YOU MUST CHOOSE!

Creature Features

Would you rather...

have a highly trained ferret that handles your postage and DVD return

OR

a highly trained chinchilla that lathers up and luffas you in the shower each morning?

Would you rather...

have a genetically engineered caterpillar that crawls to wherever you have an itch and scratches it

OR

a genetically created tiny hummingbird that cleans your nostrils, ears, belly button, and in between your toes?

YOU MUST CHOOSE!

Would you rather...

have a really smart bomb-sniffing dog who can locate anyone who would be attracted to you

OR

have a magical inch worm who can locate any g-spot?

Would you rather...

have a voodoo mouse that allowed you to drag and drop people in real life as if they were on a computer screen

OR

have a photo-editing program that actually made people change to whatever you did to them on screen?

Things to consider: How would you use your drag and drop powers? Would you use them for good or evil? What photo-editing would you do? Who would you use it on?

YOU MUST CHOOSE!

Getting Carded

Would you rather...

have a "Get out of trouble at work" card (no matter what you do, one time, you won't get in trouble)

OR

have a "Get out of trouble at home" card (same rules)?

Would you rather...

have a "Get out of jail free" card (no matter what you do, one time you will not go to jail)

OR

a "get a free Starbucks coffee a day for life" card?

Would you rather...

have a set of fake ID's that each actually create the life that they identify you as while in your wallet

OR

yellow and red cards you can give out at work (like a soccer ref) to get someone warned and fired?

YOU MUST CHOOSE!

Would you rather...

have the ability to know the answer to any trivia question, but only as long as you're completely naked

OR

have the ability to be invisible but only when spastically dancing?

Would you rather...

be able to go days without water but have a camel-like hump on your back

OR

have the saying "you are what you eat" become reality, though only affecting your hands?

Would you rather...

have a hat that styles your hair when you put it on

OR

have shoes that massage your feet with the flick of a switch?

YOU MUST CHOOSE!

Would you rather...

have seven samurai sworn to protect you **OR** seven ninjas?

5 dragons **OR** 2 wizards?

4000 hamsters **OR** 10 guidance counselors?

Would you rather...

have a pill that instantly makes you sober

OR

be able to teleport home after a night of heavy drinking no matter where you are?

Would you rather...

be permitted to backhand-slap a far-too-chipper coworker on a particularly painful Monday morning with no repercussions

OR

give your boss the finger with no repercussions?

YOU MUST CHOOSE!

Would you rather...

have one use of a morning after pill

OR

one use of a 10-years-after pill?

Would you rather...

never have to wait for an elevator

OR

always jump to the front of the list in karaoke?

YOU MUST CHOOSE!

Would you rather...

have a magic pair of glasses that allows you see what Ted Danson is seeing

OR

have magic earphones that allow you to hear what George Washington Carver's girlfriend was hearing back in time?

Would you rather...

have self-flossing teeth

OR

have an anus that manicures nails?

Would you rather...

have any member of the opposite sex's thoughts text messaged to you at any time

OR

be able to control any member of the opposite sex for up to an hour using a Sony Playstation video game controller?

YOU MUST CHOOSE!

Who would you rather have in your bedroom during sex?

a wise grizzled golf caddy who stands by the side of the bed and offers you tips on your form during sex

OR

a tennis ball boy who quickly sprints across the bed puts it back in anytime it slips out?

Who would you rather have in your bedroom during sex?

the ghost of Ed McMahon to cheer for and corroborate you ("Yesss!")

OR

a Jet Blue steward who thanks your guest for choosing you and offers them a complimentary beverage?

YOU MUST CHOOSE!

Would you rather live in a world where...

all war criminals are successfully tried and convicted

OR

where everyone who says words like "over-exaggerate" and "irregardless" without recognizing the linguistic redundancy is successfully tried and convicted?

Would you rather...

have a fountain of couth

OR

a Midas touch (everything you touch turns to a muffler)?

YOU MUST CHOOSE!

Would you rather...

have charade sex

OR

have UPS chart sex where you draw doodles that become dirty by erasing or adding lines?

Would you rather...

be fluent in Latin

OR

Pig-Latin?

YOU MUST CHOOSE!

Bird-buffs only

Would you rather...

watch a pilated woodpecker excavate a nest

OR

a bluebird feed mealworms to its brood?

Would you rather...

have a loyal entourage of game show hosts

OR

janitors?

Would you rather...

have a 50-inch ADHD TV which can't stay on any channel for more than ten seconds at a time

OR

have a big, clunky, old, rotary phone as your cell phone?

YOU MUST CHOOSE!

Would you rather...

get $1,000 anytime you punch a random person in their face
OR
get $10,000 anytime you get punched in the face?

Which of the following would you rather be able to indulge in consequence-free...

cigarettes **OR** promiscuity?

indulgent foods **OR** hard drugs?

telling crying kids in public to shut up **OR** crying and demanding a juice box whenever you don't get your way?

YOU MUST CHOOSE!

Would you rather...

be able to commune with birds to direct them exactly where to take a doo-doo

OR

have ear speakers that broadcast whatever music or sound you imagine in your head

Would you rather...

be able to speak with dead people, but only the perverts

OR

be able to read the minds of people named Ludwig?

Would you rather...

make anyone you want have a beer gut

OR

be able to literally shed pounds?

YOU MUST CHOOSE!

Would you rather...

play Wii basketball vs. Kobe Bryant

OR

that vibrating football game vs. Peyton Manning?

Would you rather...

have the ability to send unlimited text messages to yourself five minutes ago

OR

be able to sell a lame Jim Carrey movie based on the premise for $5,000,000?

YOU MUST CHOOSE!

CHAPTER THIRTY-SIX 36

DEATHS, INCONVENIENCES, AND OTHER THINGS THAT SUCK

To paraphrase Benjamin Franklin, "There are only two certainties in life: death and annoying shit." And sometimes the latter makes you wish for the former. How we bear struggle and suffering is the true test of our character. It's time to find out what you are truly made of.

Would you rather...

get Indian-burned to death

OR

noogied to death?

Would you rather...

have the Russian government determine the weather

OR

a cabal of 13-year-old girls determine your Netflix queue?

Would you rather...

have your child be raised by hyenas

OR

by pageant mothers?

YOU MUST CHOOSE!

Who would you rather have as an arch enemy?

an anteater **OR** juggler?

Bill Cosby **OR** Bill Nye (the Science Guy)

a vengeful CPA **OR** a cock-blocking warlock?

Would you rather...

commute every day through a paparazzi-infested red carpet

OR

via parade?

YOU MUST CHOOSE!

Would you rather...

be sautéed to death

OR

catapulted to your death?

Would you rather hell be...

trying to straighten impossible-to-straighten Venetian blinds

OR

a never-ending airport security line?

YOU MUST CHOOSE!

Do Try This at Home.

Would you rather...
have to talk like a robot for a whole day

OR
walk like a robot for a whole day?
Try doing each all day.

Would you rather...
have to walk with your feet never leaving the ground

OR
never be able to use the same word twice in any given 24-hour period?
Try each for a day.

Would you rather...
survive by eating lima beans and mustard for a week

OR
Brussels sprouts and prune juice?
Make a deal with your friend, designating one food
you can eat. See who can go longer.

YOU MUST CHOOSE!

Would you rather...

have as a conjoined twin, a constantly fussy baby

OR

a 1987 Ford Escort?

Would you rather...

have to drive twice the speed limit

OR

half the speed limit?

Would you rather...

be able to drink only by shotgunning cans

OR

bathe using only a turkey baster and water?

YOU MUST CHOOSE!

Would you rather...

have to brew your daily cup of coffee by peeing into the coffee maker

OR

never be able to flush your toilet?

Would you rather...

be able to only date friends of your mother's

OR

convicts with two strikes?

Would you rather...

get bedazzled to death

OR

drown in a bowl of Apple Jacks?

YOU MUST CHOOSE!

Would you rather...

emphatically boo anytime you see a postman

OR

after watching every business presentation, break out in a sarcastic slow clap and say "Well, well, well... looks like the student has become the teacher."

Would you rather...

have to wade through a dumpster full of garbage until you found a contact lens each morning

OR

have to retrieve a penny as quickly as possible in a shallow pool full of piranha?

YOU MUST CHOOSE!

Would you rather...

get literal Athlete's Foot (have one foot mutate into the foot of your favorite athelete)

OR

get literal Shingles on your back?

Would you rather...

have to wear three layers of sweats whenever you go to the beach

OR

have to wear your mom's bathing suit?

Would you rather...

drown in vomit

OR

blood?

YOU MUST CHOOSE!

Would you rather...

never again cut your finger nails

OR

never cut your hair?

Would you rather...

appear in all photos in black and white

OR

appear in all refections as Nick Nolte?

YOU MUST CHOOSE!

Would you rather...

get stuck on an elevator with gossipy girls **OR** Eastern European businessmen talking loudly on their cell phones?

skunks **OR** angry sumo wrestlers?

100 hornets **OR** (insert annoying person you know)?

Would you rather...

lay an egg and have to sit on it like a bird

OR

have to hibernate like a bear each winter from November to March?

YOU MUST CHOOSE!

Would you rather have sex with the hybrid...

LeBron James Gandolfini **OR** Jason Alexander Ovechkin?

Larry David Beckham **OR** Danica Patrick Stewart?

Lawrence Taylor Swift **OR** Carly Simon Cowell?

Kim Kardashian McKellen **OR** Rosie Perez Hilton?

Della Reese Witherspoon **OR** Sonia Sotomayor McCheese?

Things to consider: Same thing, but who would you rather have sex with?

YOU MUST CHOOSE!

Would you rather...

be caught by aliens and placed in an alien zoo

OR

be used for alien scientific research?

Would you rather...

have Vulcan ears

OR

a Vulcan personality?

Would you rather...

hear all voices as the voice of Larry King

OR

see all people as animated *Simpsons* characters?

YOU MUST CHOOSE!

Would you rather...

be allergic to all members of the opposite sex that are an "8"
or more attractive

OR

be severely allergic to all members of the opposite sex under an "8"?

Would you rather...

be unable to distinguish between sandwiches and man-eating tigers

OR

between your pet and a head of lettuce?

Would you rather...

wake up with a different stranger every morning

OR

wake up looking like a different stranger every morning?

YOU MUST CHOOSE!

Would you rather...

be the minister of tourism for Zimbabwe

OR

camp director at a camp of little, snotty, fat kids?

Would you rather...

mistake a tube of super glue for toothpaste

OR

lubricant?

YOU MUST CHOOSE!

Would you rather...

have to air your "singing in the car moments" on YouTube

OR

have to explain the terms in this book—such as "arabian goggles" and "cleveland steamer"—to your parents?

Would you rather...

get stung by a thousand wasps

OR

have to listen to El DeBarge's "In the Rhythm of the Night" 1000 times in a week?

Would you rather...

be followed by a personal heckler

OR

have a cricket that follows you around, chirping after your jokes and during all awkward silences in your conversations?

YOU MUST CHOOSE!

Would you rather...

every time you're in a car, have to hang your head out the window like a dog

OR

have to sleep curled up at the end of your parents' bed like a dog?

Would you rather...

for the rest of your life, only be able to make right turns

OR

left turns?

Would you rather...

have to hitchhike with strangers to get anywhere

OR

have to wear/use diapers and depend on strangers to change them?

YOU MUST CHOOSE!

Would you rather have to earn a living using only...

a kazoo **OR** chalk?

a dreidel **OR** six lemons?

a spatula and a jar of pearl onions **OR** your hair and a crinkled photo of Joy Behar?

Would you rather...

drink a cup of hot bacon grease

OR

of someone else's spit?

YOU MUST CHOOSE!

Would you rather...

hunt

OR

gather?

Would you rather spend a year deprived of...

water **OR** coffee?

wine **OR** dessert?

pants **OR** vowels?

YOU MUST CHOOSE!

Would you rather...

your refrigerator automatically charge your credit card with mini-bar prices

OR

have all of your Internet-viewed pornography appear on your credit card statement at a dollar a minute?

Would you rather...

swap net worth and wardrobes with Steve Jobs

OR

Bill Gates?

Would you rather...

dress exclusively in merchandise from PetSmart

OR

eat food exclusively from PetSmart?

YOU MUST CHOOSE!

37

FUN QUESTIONS FOR YOUR CHURCH YOUTH GROUP

Hey all! Here are some delightfully fun questions to get your church youth group talking. They're certain to make you think. And you just might spark a chuckle too.

Would you rather...

have to wear a scarf that your grandma knit from her pubic hair every day for a winter

OR

get hair plugs from your own pubic hair?

Would you rather...

die via bullet to head

OR

slow asphyxiation by a hairy 1970s vagina?

YOU MUST CHOOSE!

Would you rather...

lick Mo'Nique's asscrack

OR

a mound of bat guano?

Would you rather...

be caught masturbating to pictures of your ex

OR

the Hamburglar?

Would you rather...

get "dog-in-a-bath-tub'd" by Brian Williams

OR

receive an enema from Carrot Top?

Things to consider: Google it.

YOU MUST CHOOSE!

Would you rather...

be the biggest person at a little person orgy

OR

the youngest person at a nursing home orgy?

Would you rather...

have a tractor beam anus

OR

a hover vagina?

YOU MUST CHOOSE!

Would you rather wipe your ass with...

poison ivy **OR** dry ice?

a split habanero pepper **OR** your bare hand?

a steel wool pad **OR** your cat?

Would you rather...

get leg-humped by ten *Twilight* werewolves

OR

get "hot Karl'd" by the creatures in *Where the Wild Things Are?*
Things to consider: Google it.

YOU MUST CHOOSE!

Would you rather...

blindside tackle your grandma

OR

give her ten seconds of mouth to mouth?

YOU MUST CHOOSE!

Would you rather...

suck on your high school English teacher's nipples

OR

frog intestines?

Would you rather...

find a sex video of your best friend and your boyfriend/girlfriend

OR

of your parents?

YOU MUST CHOOSE!

Would you rather...

watch a stripper who was 80-years-old **OR** 400 pounds?

who keeps farting audibly and potently **OR** who looks a little like your mom?

who dances '80s breakdancing **OR** does a Stomp routine?

Would you rather...

play strip poker with the cast of *The View*
OR
60 Minutes?

YOU MUST CHOOSE!

Would you rather...

delicately place your penis in the mouth of a cow

OR

in a French fry fryer?

Would you rather...

receive a Cleveland Steamer from your partner

OR

a $5,000 parking ticket?

YOU MUST CHOOSE!

WHO'D YOU RATHER...?
PART 2:
ELECTRIC BOOGALOO

Still looking for that perfect somebody? The yin to your sexual yang? Well, your yang need not be alone much longer. Luckily there are plenty more people, robots, mascots, cartoons, and inanimate objects to sift through. So keep plugging away until you find Mr. or Mrs. Right (or at least Mr. or Mrs. Right *Angle*!) Wait, no... that's not how it goes.

Would you rather...

have sex with Sam Worthington's paraplegic marine character in *Avatar* **OR** his blue alien avatar?

Prince Harry **OR** Prince William?

Mr. Rogers **OR** Captain Kangaroo?

YOU MUST CHOOSE!

Would you rather have sex with...

any four cast members from the show *Glee*, then have them do a musical number about it **OR** any four cast members of *Saturday Night Live*, then have them perform a comedy sketch about it?

have sex with your choice of Reese Witherspoon/Jason Bateman and have everybody know about it **OR** have sex with your choice of Megan Fox/Johnny Depp and have no one know about it?

YOU MUST CHOOSE!

(im)Perfect Partners

Would you rather...

have a sex partner who always ejaculates prematurely after one minute **OR** one who ejaculates 2 days postmaturely wherever they are?

have sex with Penelope Cruz if she spoke dirty in a Spanish accent **OR** Heidi Klum if she spoke dirty in a frightening German accent?

Barry Manilow if he then wrote you a love song **OR** Eminem if he then wrote a hateful rap about you?

have sex with Salma Hayek's body but with your face on it **OR** with your body with Salma Hayek's face (genitals remain female)?

YOU MUST CHOOSE!

Would you rather...

be attacked by ninjas while having sex with a supermodel

OR

vice-versa?

Would you rather...

have cowgirl sex with a missionary

OR

missionary sex with a cowgirl?
Things to consider: conversion, spurs

YOU MUST CHOOSE!

Would you rather watch a discovered sex tape with...

Brad Pitt and Angelina Jolie **OR** Barack and Michelle Obama?

Yao Ming and Christina Ricci **OR** Tracy Morgan and Vanessa Hudgens?

the contestants on the last *Biggest Loser* (pre-weight loss) in an orgy **OR** your parents?

a camel and a koala bear **OR** two deaf people?

Johnny Depp and Julia Child **OR** the Gumbel brothers and Eliza Dushku?

Would you rather...

screw a janitor on a space ship

OR

an astronaut in a janitor's closet?

YOU MUST CHOOSE!

Which threesome partners would you rather have?

former couple Padma Lakshmi and Salman Rushdie **OR** Woody Allen and Soon Yi?

Jerry Lewis and Juliette Lewis **OR** Tom Brady and Mrs. Brady?

Sienna Miller and Dennis Miller **OR** Halle Berry and Frankenberry?

YOU MUST CHOOSE!

Would you rather...

have sex with this guy

OR

this guy?

YOU MUST CHOOSE!

Would you rather...

have sex with Abe Lincoln

OR

George Washington?

Would you rather...

have sex with Ashley Olsen if she lost 50 pounds

OR

Kirstie Alley if she gained 50 pounds?

Would you rather...

have sex with someone who you are able to apply Photoshop effects to in real life

OR

someone who could do an impression of anyone perfectly?

Things to consider: Dragon wings would look awesome!; possible impressions: porn stars, movie stars, Don Rickles, your old girlfriend/boyfriend

YOU MUST CHOOSE!

Would you rather...

play spin the bottle with the cast of *Baywatch* **OR** the cast of *Gilligan's Island*?

the cast of the new *90210* **OR** the old *90210*?

with the crew of *Star Trek: The Next Generation* **OR** *Star Trek: Voyager*?
Things to consider: Vulcans possess nearly three times the strength of humans, *Voyager's* Holodeck has slightly more advanced graphics than *Enterprise's*, 7 of 9's nature is to comply with the will of the collective, Counselor Troy is only half Betazoid ... y'know, if you're into that sort of thing.

YOU MUST CHOOSE!

Mash-ups!

Which of the following hybrids would you rather have sex with?

Kirk Cameron Diaz **OR** Tera Patrick Dempsey?

Rachael Ray Lewis **OR** Liv Tyler Perry?

Robert Blake Lively **OR** Nate Hayden Panettiere?

YOU MUST CHOOSE!

Would you rather...

have sex with everyone who has ever held a Guinness World Record for a physical oddity or deformity

OR

all of the people who have ever appeared as a guest on the
Jerry Springer Show?

Things to consider: fat twins on motorcycles, long nails dude, World's most rotund knees guy

Would you rather...

have sex with a half-sized J-Lo

OR

a double-sized J-Lo?

Would you rather...

have sex with Jessica Biel but get crabs

OR

make out with Meredith Vieira and get a free Big Gulp?

YOU MUST CHOOSE!

Would you rather...

have sex with the Quaker Oats mascot in a bed of his oatmeal

OR

Uncle Ben in a bed of his rice?

Things to consider: Both will be done in under 5 minutes.

Would you rather...

have sex with Emeril Lagasse and then have him cook a four-course meal for you

OR

Christian Bale and then have him chew you out for not getting something right?

YOU MUST CHOOSE!

Would you rather have sex with...

this woman

OR

this woman?

YOU MUST CHOOSE!

Would you rather...

have sex with Grace Park **OR** Mila Kunis?

Jenna Jameson **OR** Tila Tequila?

Elizabeth Berkley **OR** Elisabeth Hasselbeck?

Tiffani-Amber Thiessen **OR** Tiffani Thiessen?

Would you rather...

have an orgy with an NFL team after they've just won the Super Bowl
OR
after they've just lost the Super Bowl?

YOU MUST CHOOSE!

Would you rather...

have sex with Kristen Stewart from *Twilight* **OR** Anna Paquin from *True Blood*?

with Jorja Fox on the set of *CSI* **OR** one of the models on the set of the *Price is Right*?

with a woman with no hair **OR** a woman with a soul patch?

the cast of *Jersey Shore* **OR** the creatures in Jabba the Hutt's fortress?

Would you rather...

have sex with Johnny Depp with facial hair **OR** clean-shaven Johnny Depp?

Alan Greenspan with a 12-inch schlong **OR** Derek Jeter with a one-incher?

Keith Richards **OR** an Oompa-Loompa?

YOU MUST CHOOSE!